CONSERVATION BY DESIGN

This publication was supported by:

Rhode Island Resource Conservation and Development Area, Inc.
and U.S.D.A. Forest Service

World Wildlife Fund

The Knoll Group

Peter Joseph Gallery

Edmund A. Stanley, Jr.

Freeport-McMoRan Company

Susan and Robert Bruce

Martin Guitar Company

Anonymous private donor

CONSERVATION BY DESIGN

Scott Landis

Editor

Museum of Art, Rhode Island School of Design
Woodworkers Alliance for Rainforest Protection

Cover photo: Orcas Island, Washington, by Scott Landis
All photos on pp. 76-147 by Dean Powell, unless otherwise noted.

Published in conjunction with the exhibition Conservation by Design (October 29, 1993–January 16, 1994)

First printing: October 1993

International Standard Book Number: 0-9638593-0-7

Library of Congress Catalog Card Number: 93-61458

Woodworkers Alliance for Rainforest Protection
One Cottage Street
Easthampton, MA 01027

Museum of Art
Rhode Island School of Design
Two College Street
Providence, RI 02903

Contents

Foreword

Woodworking, and in particular the creation of custom furniture, represents a rare conjunction of beauty evolved by living Nature and beauty contrived by the human mind. As the essays and entries within this catalogue express so well, the making of furniture is also a record of history. It tells us about trade expansion around the world, about fashion, and periodically, and delightfully, about creative genius.

The connection of art to conservation is this: a master craftsman can work a piece of art out of common wood, but he reaches a new level when he applies that skill to various, imaginatively chosen species of wood, some of which may have been previously unemployed, some rare, some unfortunately pushed to the edge of extinction by forces beyond the woodworker's reach.

I am a biologist whose entire career has been focused on biodiversity and whose knowledge of fine furniture is limited to untutored admiration. Yet woodworkers and I share a common interest. Artists working in wood are natural conservationists. Their expertise extends to relevant aspects of biodiversity. When tree species become unattainably rare or extinct, woodworkers are in the position of painters or sculptors who are denied certain pigments and surfaces. That is just what is happening, and at an accelerating rate.

The problem is especially serious in the case of tropical woods, although it is no less tragic when temperate forests are threatened with extinction. The rainforests harbor a majority of the world's tree species, and many local floras are legendary in their diversity. The known world record is held by a forest tract on the coast of southern Bahia in Brazil, where, in 1993, 450 tree species were reported to be found on 1 hectare (2.5 acres). There are 700 native tree species in all of North America.

Tragically, the treasure house is shrinking fast. By the late 1970s, the rainforests were being reduced worldwide by cutting and burning at a rate of slightly less than one percent per year. By the late 1980s, the annual rate of clearing had doubled. Today less than half of the world's original rainforest remains. It occupies about six percent of Earth's land surface, roughly equal to the contiguous forty-eight states of the United States. The cover removed annually is about equal to the area of the state of Florida. Many of the most threatened tropical forests are unfortunately also among the most diverse. The Bahia coastal tract, for example, is one of the most heavily lumbered in the world.

Hundreds of independent studies on many groups of organisms, including flowering plants, have shown that a large reduction in area of habitat is virtually always accompanied by extinction of species. To be more precise, the number of species declines as the third to sixth root of the area lost. The exact degree depends on the place and the kind of organisms under consideration: whether, for example, the birds of Hawaii or the trees of Central America. A typical value, reasonably accurate in many cases, is the fourth root. It can be easily remembered by this rule of thumb: a habitat loss of ninety percent eventually brings about a fifty percent loss of the number of species. By this rule, the rate of global annual reduction of tropical rainforest, 1.8 percent, indicates an eventual extinction of 0.5 percent of the number of species.

There are plenty of examples of woody plant species on the edge of extinction. Some tree species in the tiny forest reserves of western Ecuador are known from only one or two individuals, and are unlikely to reproduce further. In the black-humor notation of conservation biologists, they are classified as the "living dead." By 1986, the species *Banara vanderbiltii,* a small tree of Puerto Rico's moist limestone forests, had declined in number to two plants growing on a farm near Bayamon. At the eleventh hour, cuttings were made and are now successfully growing in the Fairchild Tropical Garden in Miami, Florida. In Hawaii, the sole living individual of *Kokia cookei* survives as a graft on the trunk of another species of *Kokia.*

As tropical forests are destroyed, they are being replaced in a few places by new plantings. But only rarely do the species in the reforestation effort include elements of the original flora. In no case

of which I am aware is an attempt being made to restore the full diversity of species. More typically, one to several exotic species are introduced, chosen for their rapid growth and commercial values as sources of pulpwood and mass-construction materials.

There are many reasons for conserving the biological diversity of forests. One of the most compelling is their aesthetic value. But that is an elusive concept, not measured in dollars and cents. It is best expressed by example. By creating art from biodiversity, woodworkers provide one of the most striking of such examples, and their voices as conservationists will be heard.

Edward O. Wilson

Preface

Since the founding of Rhode Island School of Design (RISD) in 1877, the mission of the school and its Museum of Art has been "the instruction of artisans" and "the general advancement of public Art education, by the exhibition of works of Art." Both the school and museum have grown significantly since then, with enrollment now at approximately 1,900 and the museum's encyclopedic collection containing approximately 100,000 works of art.

Conservation by Design is the latest in a series of collaborative efforts made in the past decade between the museum curators and those members of the RISD faculty who had the desire to address a particular style, material, or technique by means of original works of art. Recent exhibitions focusing on furniture design have ranged from the conceptual (Furniture, Furnishings: Subject and Object, 1984) and technological (Bentwood, 1984) to the historical (Cabinetmakers and Collectors, 1986; Furniture in Print, 1988) and contemporary (Contemporary Crafts: A Decade of Collecting, 1990).

A decade ago, RISD's commitment to acquiring outstanding examples of contemporary studio furniture was unusual among American museums, but it was the logical complement to the school's distinguished Furniture Design Program, established in 1962 and led by Tage Frid, and the museum's renowned collection of eighteenth- and nineteenth-century furniture. Since then, the studio-furniture movement has flourished worldwide. Following the early example of Boston's Museum of Fine Arts, major American museums are now actively commissioning contemporary furniture, while specious distinctions between art and craft gradually disappear.

The idea for this exhibition was first proposed to the Museum of Art three years ago by Seth Stem and Rosanne Somerson of RISD's Furniture Design Program upon Seth's return from the founding conference of the Woodworkers Alliance for Rainforest Protection (WARP) at the University of Massachusetts in Amherst. RISD has worked with WARP and the United States Forest Service's Rhode Island Resource Conservation and Development Area with the hope that a museum exhibition with dual emphasis on artists' responsibilities for their materials and patrons' for their patterns of consumption could intensify awareness of global conservation issues, promote responsible art and design, and still provide the museum-going public with aesthetic enjoyment.

Finally, it is appropriate that the opening of this exhibition coincide with the inauguration of the Daphne Farago Wing of the Museum of Art, whose new galleries for contemporary art ensure RISD's ability to continue to educate artists and designers and to promote public art education well into the next century.

Thomas W. Leavitt
Director
Museum of Art
Rhode Island School of Design

Acknowledgments

As is true of any museum exhibition and publication whose production spans three years, Conservation by Design has benefited from the generous assistance of a number of individuals and associations.

Neither exhibition nor catalogue would have been possible without the generous support of the Rhode Island Resource Conservation and Development Area (RI RC & D), in cooperation with the Rhode Island Department of Environmental Management (DEM, Division of Forest Environment) and the United States Department of Agriculture's Forest Service (USFS). Art museums are not customarily within the purview of professional forest managers and ecologists, and yet by means of this exhibition, catalogue, and accompanying educational programs, RI RC & D has enabled us to work with artists to enhance museum visitors' awareness of wood as a renewable resource and to introduce a potentially new audience to the complex issues of resource management. We are especially grateful to Kathleen Leddy, formerly with RI RC & D, and Bryan Wolfenden, executive director; Carolyn Weymouth and Jay Aron of DEM; Thomas Dupree, Rhode Island state forester; and Mary Hallett, of the USFS, who served as a conservation advisor to the jury and assisted the curators with interpretive materials for the exhibition.

Generous assistance for the exhibition catalogue has also come from the World Wildlife Fund (WWF), The Knoll Group, Peter Joseph Gallery, Susan and Robert Bruce, the Freeport-McMoRan Company, Edmund A. Stanley Jr., and the Martin Guitar Company. In particular, we wish to thank Mike Kiernan of WWF and George Wilmot of Knoll for their encouragement and support. We also wish to thank Lorry Dudley and Peter Joseph Gallery, Peter Dudley, and Peter Garlington for their timely assistance with furniture shipped from New York. We are also grateful to Judith Zuidema and Kirsten Williams of Knoll, John Economaki and Jill Palamountain of Bridge City Tool Works, and Dick Boak of Martin Guitar for arranging loans of their companies' products, as well as to Al Barrenechea of Royal Mahogany Products, who provided Portico materials. Once all shipments had arrived, Dean Powell successfully transformed one of the museum's oldest galleries into a state-of-the-art photography studio and completed all photography and processing with remarkable efficiency and results.

The board of directors of the Woodworkers Alliance for Rainforest Protection (WARP) has supported this project from the beginning. They directed this publication and worked with the Museum of Art, Rhode Island School of Design (RISD), to shape the content of the exhibition it accompanies. Silas Kopf served as juror and Ivan Ussach as conservation advisor to the jury. John Curtis, partner in The Luthier's Mercantile, compiled the list of properties of lesser-known species that appears on pp. 148-151, and Dr. Richard Jagels, professor of forest biology at the University of Maine, reviewed all the scientific names that appear in the text. Wood samples used in the exhibition and photographed for the catalogue were provided by EcoTimber International and Sea Star Trading. Nina Maurer helped raise funds for production of the catalogue.

At RISD, Kenneth Hunnibel, professor of industrial design, encouraged the development of the relationship between WARP and RISD that led to this exhibition. Mary Belden Brown, director of corporate and foundation relations, and her assistant, Ronn Smith, made a significant effort in seeking funds for this project. Alan Holoubek and Elizabeth Lee, graduate students in the Furniture Design Program, and Michael Frankel, a museum intern, were valuable assistants.

Members of the museum staff who deserve special thanks are Louann Skorupa, registrar, who arranged for the shipping and delivery of over seventy objects from around the world; James Swan, head of installation, and his good-natured crew; Judith A. Singsen, museum editor; and Debra Pelletier, who carried out numerous clerical tasks. When this collaborative venture was first proposed to RISD museum curators, former director Franklin Robinson eagerly embraced and supported the concept. We wish to thank his successor, Thomas Leavitt, for his continued support and wise counsel as the project took shape.

Any success of the catalogue is due in large measure to the thoughtful and provocative contributions of the essay authors: Edward O. Wilson, Edward S. Cooke, Jr. (who also lent his insights to the jury), John Makepeace, Silas Kopf, Robert O'Neal, Timothy J. Synnott, Laura K. Snook, and Roy Keene. Their work, as well as the voluminous artists' statements, was focused, refined, and coordinated by the editorial skills of Deborah Cannarella. The catalogue designer, Jeanne Criscola, was enlisted early in the process, and she, along with Debra Della Camera and Suzan Shutan, worked tirelessly to weave an elegant, integrated whole from a vast quantity of visual and textual materials. She also recruited the printer, Sam Lindberg, of W.E. Andrews Co., whose efforts in procuring paper and overseeing the printing have paid off handsomely in the end.

Finally, the artists themselves deserve our profound thanks for submitting thoughtful, innovative, and beautiful works of art for exhibition. Their tangible responses to the theme of this exhibition represent creative approaches to responsible design and consumption, conservation, and ultimately, renewal.

Thomas S. Michie
Jayne E. Stokes
Department of Decorative Arts
Museum of Art, Rhode Island School of Design

Rosanne Somerson
Graduate Furniture Design Program
Rhode Island School of Design

Seth Stem
Industrial Design Department
Rhode Island School of Design

Scott Landis
Woodworkers Alliance for Rainforest Protection

> Human history
> becomes more
> and more
> a race between
> education
> and catastrophe.
>
> — H.G. Wells

Introductions

Odd as it may sound, one of the primary roles of educators is to create confusion. Learning results from breaking down the preconceived notions that students have collected from a long line of influences, beliefs that often make complex problems seem simple and that can overshadow new discoveries. Ideally, designers should be innovators, anticipating the needs of a future generation and, through new responses to specific issues, helping to redefine that future. The educator's role in the design disciplines is to challenge students to understand the breadth of questions and to provide them with the skills and conceptual tools to find their own solutions.

As we approach the end of a century and of a millennium, design educators reflect on where we stand as a culture and anticipate the role of tomorrow's designers. Designers affect our culture directly through the specifications they assign to manufacturers and through their products, which dictate contemporary behaviors. Think about the changes in everyday rituals brought about by microwave ovens, telephone-answering machines, and remote-controlled VCRs.

As John Ruskin, the nineteenth-century English critic and writer, stated, "Education does not mean teaching people what they do not know; it means teaching them to behave as they do not behave." By raising students' awareness of the implications of design choices, whether they relate to material choices, the longevity of objects, the byproducts of manufacturing, or psychological experience, educators help students to better understand that the way we behave as a culture affects our entire planet today and the one that our children will know tomorrow.

In the Furniture Design Program in the Industrial Design Department at Rhode Island School of Design (RISD) there has been a surge of concern about the relationship of environmental and design issues. Most of our students are optimistic about the future and want to create objects that will leave the world a better place.

Students are asking a lot of difficult, thought-provoking questions. They want to be responsible in their choice of materials, but they don't always know how to be. At RISD, we have devoted a great deal of time to experimenting with less conventional materials or techniques as alternatives to exotic woods, even trying to compete with the luscious qualities inherent in these woods. Students carve and decorate surfaces on readily available local species, cast materials into transparent mediums, substitute found objects or recycled materials for new lumber.

Knowing that the answers are not simple, faculty try to at least heighten awareness about the questions by presenting many views. We encourage students to research the sources of the materials they use and to understand the impact of working in certain methods. Often they are frustrated because few lumberyards can answer their questions. Some students, already burdened with the high expenses of education, find the higher prices of lesser-known species prohibitive. Some have difficulty finding woods that will be dry enough to use while they are still in school. Some choose to work in resins, metals, and plastics, as alternatives to expensive or endangered woods, and then find that these materials may be as ecologically threatening, and, in some cases, dangerous or even carcinogenic to the makers.

Student artists and designers are keenly aware of these dilemmas, and the educational institution can provide a testing ground for exploring options. Not unlike a scientist, the artist-designer sets out to solve a problem armed with a hypothesis and through a number of explorations hopes to arrive at a satisfying solution. The scientific process may be more concrete, but the artist-designer's investigation may reach the esoteric and personal, even the spiritual. Artists aim to transform the commonplace into something magical through aesthetic excellence.

When I laud the confusion in our institution, I am really praising an environment that encourages change. There have already been successes, as students discover ways to transform the common into the beautiful and the useful, or as they ask poignant questions through the conceptual content in their work. Our student work is

widely published and exhibited and therefore reaches a large public. The Industrial Design Department has many ties to industry through special projects, and some student work has already had an impact on industry.

Through this exhibition, based on the great need for change and for increased awareness, we all are working to educate each other. Perhaps we can win the race that H.G. Wells describes, as we guide our future history farther away from catastrophe.

Rosanne Somerson
Acting Head
Graduate Furniture Design Program
Rhode Island School of Design

The idea for an exhibition promoting wood as a sustainable resource had its origins in the 1990 conference of the Woodworkers Alliance for Rainforest Protection (WARP) in Amherst, Massachusetts, which I attended. The air was charged with the enthusiasm of the many people there who wanted to make a positive contribution. A great deal of information was shared, and after considerable discussion about raising public awareness through a furniture exhibition, there was a feverish exhange of ideas and phone numbers. The curators of the Museum of Art liked the proposal, WARP and RISD joined forces, and this project was born.

WARP and RISD combined their lists of people who might contribute thoughtfully to an important exhibition of this kind. Rhode Island is rich in well-trained furnituremakers, designers, and craftspeople. For decades, RISD has been one of this country's foremost educational centers for design, and we at RISD hoped that our alumni and faculty, along with those of other schools, as well as individual designers and craftspeople, would provide a good foundation for an exhibition addressing the issue of sustainable wood.

Design affects objects in many ways: in terms of the materials consumed, the conservation and manufacturing processes, and the public perception of what is or is not acceptable in a commercial product. Through this exhibition, we hope to bring a new consciousness to those who use and enjoy wood. We hope that the young designers we are now educating at RISD will develop a fuller awareness of conservation in design and that, individually and collectively, they will have a positive impact on the way that wood and other materials are specified and used in the future.

Seth Stem
Associate Professor
Industrial Design Department
Rhode Island School of Design

Last spring, I attended a gathering of woodworkers to discuss the future of craft. Toshio Odate, a sculptor and maker of Japanese sliding doors, trained in a traditional old-world apprenticeship, defined craftsmanship this way: "Craftsman," Toshio said, "is one hundred percent social service. Society asks and you make it." Well, for the most part, society isn't asking. For the last century, and more, craft has been increasingly consigned to the margins of economic life.

The functional and sculptural art work in this catalogue and in the Conservation by Design exhibition is no exception. It is almost entirely nonessential. We don't need turners to make our bowls any more than we need blacksmiths to forge our hinges or tailors to make our clothes.

Alongside this marginalization of craft, we have also witnessed the reduction of the world's great forests. We have cut, fished, and mined our way around the earth and met ourselves coming over the other side. There is virtually no Amazonian or Siberian vastness that we cannot loot. We know where the forest ends.

Strictly speaking, we don't *need* craft, or perhaps even forests, to survive. We are learning how to grow trees like carrots. What we do need is to preserve a place for craft and forests in our lives, both as individuals and as a culture. They are an important part of what makes us human.

The participants in this exhibition begin from that common point, acknowledging the fragility of the world's forests and the importance of craft and design in our lives. Less clear is the relationship between resource consumption, craft, and design. What role can artists and craftspeople play in reversing a drama that is unfolding on a global stage? What responsibility do craftspeople share for the depletion of our forest resources? And what can we do about it?

The relationship of "gourmet" wood use and forest destruction has a long history. The Romans plundered sandarac pine (*Callitris articulata*) in North Africa to build exquisite tables and, in the process, helped to create a desert. As Silas Kopf suggests in his essay on p. 35, a French cabinetmaker—called an *ébéniste*, a worker of ebony (*Diospyros* spp.)—would be hard pressed today to find a decent specimen of that tropical timber. Luthiers bemoan the sorry state of Brazilian rosewood (*Dalbergia nigra*) and its recent listing as an endangered species. Caribbean mahogany (*Swietenia mahagoni*), which was one of the most valuable tropical timbers in trade for three hundred years, has been commercially extinct for most of this century, and we're making serious inroads into mainland supplies of Honduras mahogany (*S. macrophylla*).

It is not within the power of artists or craftspeople to stem the tide of environmental degradation. The causes are many, and the actual consumption of timber by artisans is probably negligible. But if politically correct bowls and cabinets won't save the rainforest, they will help tell the story.

In wood and in trees, foresters, biologists, and environmentalists share a natural, common interest with artists, designers, furniture historians, and even business leaders. That they rarely talk to one another explains why the environment and the economy seem to be so often at odds. One of the principal goals of this exhibition—and this catalogue in particular—is to reach out across institutional and habitual boundaries to stimulate the discussion. Another goal is to engage the public in the dialogue.

A lot has happened in the few short years since 1990, when the seed of this exhibition was planted at the founding conference of the Woodworkers Alliance for Rainforest Protection. The wood-certification movement, which was then in its infancy, has been gaining experience and gathering steam. The number of retailers who were selling wood from well-managed or certified forest projects could be counted on one hand; now, there is a growing network across the country. Large companies who were only flirting with the idea of responsible forestry have linked some of their reputation and their profit to the concept. What's more, the very notion of "sustainable development"—however misconstrued and abused that complicated buzzword has become—has begun to take root in popular culture. The urgent needs of forest dwellers and timber-producing nations are being balanced as never before with the interests of industry and the compelling call to preserve diverse species and wild places. There is hardly an environmental organization or a wood-based industry today that does not at least pay lip service to the validity of these competing claims.

It may seem presumptuous to count these small successes when the task remains so daunting. But of all the causes for hope, the greatest may be found in these new collaborations. Conservation by Design demonstrates the kind of interdisciplinary, cooperative approach that will be essential, on a much larger scale, to the resolution of our most intractable environmental and human crises. By combining the resources of a premier design institution and a highly respected art museum with a grassroots environmental organization, we offer a modest template for change.

Museums are conservationists at heart. Their primary role is to preserve and interpret the past. It is in the nature of schools and education to look forward. An active environmental organization must be firmly rooted in the present, developing strategies that will influence public policy and opinion. In Conservation by Design, we have attempted to weave these three strands together—past, present, and future—to shed new light on an ancient dilemma. It is an effort to cultivate and inspire the kind of vision that occasionally enables us to reach beyond ourselves and the narrow, parochial confines of our respective cultures and institutions.

Education is central to both sponsors: the Museum of Art, Rhode Island School of Design, and the Woodworkers Alliance for Rainforest Protection. But education is no substitute for understanding, and understanding divorced from action is sterile. At its best, the work in this exhibition may offer a catalyst for change simply by demonstrating the power of a craft that embraces a difficult idea and recognizes its own social context. In their artists' statement, John and Carolyn Grew-Sheridan write that "overcoming inertia can be the most difficult step in any significant project, process, or journey." Our feet are on the path.

Scott Landis

President

Woodworkers Alliance for Rainforest Protection

CONSERVATION IN DESIGN

Edward S. Cooke, Jr.

John Makepeace

Silas Kopf

Seth Stem

Robert O'Neal

Beyond Aesthetics
Wood choice in historical furniture

Edward S. Cooke, Jr.

*F*urniture historians have always shown an interest in the material with which joiners and cabinetmakers worked. Scholars have linked stylistic periods with specific types of wood: the age of oak gave way to the age of walnut, which in turn gave way to the age of mahogany.[1]

This traditional approach focuses on the aesthetic qualities of the wood and its grain and the formal qualities of the visible mass. Furthermore, the assumptions of this evolutionary sequence were based only on the most expensive and stylish furniture. In the 1950s, American furniture historians began to examine the varieties of primary wood and to analyze secondary woods, but they did so to confirm regional attributions or to define the work of a particular shop. Wood identification has thus remained more of a tool of connoisseurship for collectors than an analytical tool for artifactual interpretation.[2]

Chest of drawers with doors, Boston, Massachusetts (1650-1670). White oak, red oak, chestnut, eastern white pine, soft maple, black walnut, cedar, cedrela, snakewood, rosewood, lignum vitae. (H: 48⁷/₈ in., W: 45³/₄ in., D: 23³/₄ in.)

The sophisticated form, architectural facade, dovetailed drawer construction and high degree of interior finish mark this chest as one of the finest and most important examples of high-style, London-influenced joinery made in the colonies. The maker embellished the red- and white-oak carcase with the following imported woods: cedrela for carcase moldings; snakewood for the spindles on the upper section and the panels on drawer and door fronts; rosewood for the spindles on the lower section; and lignum vitae for the drawer pulls on the upper section. (Yale University Art Gallery, The Mabel Brady Garvan Collection [1930.2109].)

Our developing understanding about sustainable forests, responsible harvesting, lesser-known species, environmentally and economically efficient woodworking, and "silvicultural correctness" presents an opportunity to examine historical wood usage in a broader context. Woodworkers have often had some choice between local and imported materials, and various factors influenced that choice: availability of different woods, intended market, traditions of craftsmen from another region, labor systems, and, of course, fashion. Rather than ask only from what woods is the piece of furniture made, it would be helpful to ask: what do the primary or secondary woods reveal about the market or about the organization of work in specific places or at specific times? Who controls the supply of materials? How do world trade patterns affect materials? These questions are founded upon the importance of examining design and style in relationship to social, political, and economic forces. The choice of woods is embedded within the values of a society and can reveal issues about cultural cohesion, social dominance, or even labor exploitation.[3]

There are both cultural and environmental reasons for the dominance of oak in American seventeenth-century New England furniture. Oak had been the preferred wood in postmedieval England at the time of the Great Migration in the 1630s, and many immigrant craftsmen in the Colonies sought to preserve their familiar tradition. Provided with a plentiful supply of red and white oak (*Quercus* spp.), which had to be cleared to establish arable land, immigrant joiners used familiar woods to build familiar forms based upon the regional traditions in which they were trained.

The preparation of these woods, however, reveals the influence of a different environment. The English joiners and woodworkers carefully pit-sawed or frame-sawed wood to make efficient use of their increasingly scarce timber. The plentiful supply of wood and the absence of an established sawyers' guild allowed colonial joiners to favor riving, a technique that was fast and easy, but wasteful of wood.

The colonists' reduction of the forests through clearing, lumbering, and wasteful woodworking was justified at the time as the "progress of cultivation." In fact, many early colonists did not understand and even ridiculed Native Americans' more efficient and responsible use of forest resources.[4]

Colonists in New England also found extensive forests of tall, straight white pine (*Pinus strobus*). The conifer became the basis of a thriving lumber economy, particularly in the region north of Boston, and had an impact on wood processing and furnituremaking. Water-powered sawmills, established as early as the late 1630s, became the dominant method of preparing boards. The availability of pine, water-sawn boards stimulated an innovation: the substitution of pine board tops for paneled oak tops.

Although oak remained the preferred material for tables and case furniture until the end of the seventeenth century, the importance of trade to Boston's economy during the middle of the century led to an aspiring merchant class eager to distinguish itself with fashionable furnishings. In addition to importing English and European ceramics, having local silversmiths imitate styles from Portugal, France, or England, and hiring masons or joiners to build houses in the Lowlands Mannerist tradition, the increasingly cosmopolitan elite wanted to distinguish themselves through the ownership and display of furniture with decorative woods.[5] Trade with the West Indies, the Americas, and even Madeira and the other wine islands off the coast of Spain brought new varieties of woods, such as cedrela (*Cedrela odorata* from Central America or the Caribbean), ebony (*Diospyros* spp., probably from East Asia via the Dutch West Indies), snakewood (*Piratinera guianensis* from Dutch Guiana), and rosewood (*Dalbergia nigra*). The joiners used these woods primarily on large cases pieces for ornamental details, such as moldings and applied turnings.

Renewed British interest in the colonies during the 1670s led to the development of a new fashion among the colonial elite. English officials visiting the colonies stimulated a market for the latest British styles of cane chairs, burl-veneered case furniture, and Baroque-influenced turning. A new wave of English craftsmen migrated to the colonies in the last quarter of the seventeenth century and was patronized by these English officials, as well as by aspiring native merchants and magistrates. While New England craftsmen replicated middle-class London fashion in local woods—

cane chairs of maple (*Acer* spp.) rather than beech (*Fagus grandifolia*), case furniture with white pine carcases veneered with black walnut (*Juglans nigra*)—the plentiful supply of black walnut in the Middle Colonies (mainly Pennsylvania, New York, and Virginia) permitted more extensive use of solid walnut. Burl or figured veneers were popular for drawer fronts, but solid walnut was used for carcase sides. The Boston makers also used solid walnut for the legs of tables and case furniture rather than following the English convention of staining a common wood. Boston's trade with the emerging Middle Colonies in the early eighteenth century accounted for the great quantity of walnut drop-leaf tables, case furniture, and chairs throughout this period.[6]

In the second quarter of the eighteenth century, as New York and Philadelphia grew and developed their own regional furniture markets, Boston merchants were less able to purchase walnut and sell finished furniture. Again mirroring the changing fashion in England, merchants from Boston and other areas of New England began to import mahogany (*Swietenia mahagoni*) from the Caribbean region. Lumber merchants in Boston and Newport, Rhode Island, and in even smaller ports such as New London, Connecticut, became suppliers for local craftsmen. New England cabinetmakers in port towns began making expensive furniture predominantly in mahogany; stylish furniture in the Middle Colonies was made of mahogany as well as walnut.

The surviving furniture made in the third quarter of the eighteenth century reveals the distinctive view that the tropical primary wood did not possess inherent value. Especially in Boston there is a wasteful use of the material in the expensive bombé and blockfront case pieces: solid four- or five-inch-thick boards were sawed, adzed, and planed to produce the rich masses of this well-known body of work. Much of the material was lost as waste, indicating that time was more important than material. The emphasis on saving time is also evident in the interior joinery, which is often expedient and lacking in finish. Local secondary woods such as white pine for drawer linings, white cedar (*Chamaecyparis thyoides*) for drawer bottoms, and birch (*Betula* spp.) for upholstery frames reveal the Boston cabinetmakers' reliance on regional suppliers outside of the city. Boston furniture manifests the economic difficulties faced by that port's craftsmen during the years of prolonged stagflation in the middle of the eighteenth century. They had to produce quickly to make a living, yet they also had to produce showy furniture for the few merchants who were able to make profits during these years.[7]

In Newport, a stable craft structure based on family dynasties and a supportive merchant community led to better-built furniture that demonstrated concern for the expansion and contraction of the materials. Merchants supplied high-quality, dense mahogany that contrasted with the lighter, blemished wood found on many of the Boston pieces. The handling of the tropical wood also reveals a more economical approach in Newport: the blocking for drawer fronts and desk fronts is applied and the blocking on bookcase doors is achieved with paneling. Interiors of Newport work often incorporate chestnut (*Castanea dentata*). Was chestnut used because it was a common, local, ring-porous wood similar in structure and working qualities to the oak used by English-trained craftsmen working in Rhode Island, because its stability made it well suited for drawer linings, or because local people could easily rive it and provide a constant supply?[8]

The local economy particularly influenced inland New England where furnituremakers participated in local or regional economies based upon the exchange of goods and services. These regions were not tied by entrepreneurial traders to lands that supplied exotic species, although they were usually aware of fashion and style in other regions. The widespread use of cherry (*Prunus serotina*) as the primary wood in Connecticut and of maple in New Hampshire is fundamentally the result of

Desk and bookcase, Boston, Massachusetts (1770-1790). Mahogany, eastern white pine. (H: 95⁷/₈ in., W: 45¹/₈ in., D: 24¹/₄ in.)

The use of large panels of book-matched, crotch mahogany and of blocking cut from solid wood document the wasteful practices of Boston's work in mahogany. (Yale University Art Gallery, bequest of Doris M. Brixey [1984.32.29].)

these local supply networks. There were regional variations in how the local joiners finished these native hardwoods: near ports such as Portsmouth, New Hampshire, and New London, joiners often favored stained curly maple to simulate the richness of figured mahogany. In western New England, joiners were more apt to use maple or cherry with a resinous finish but no stain. The popularity of the differing types of secondary woods—oak and yellow poplar (*Liriodendron tulipifera*) in western Connecticut, white pine in New Hampshire, and chestnut in eastern Connecticut and Rhode Island—also points to the strength of these local networks.[9]

After the Revolution, the most noticeable change in materials was the widespread use of veneer. While scholars have often pointed out the influence of technological improvements in the sawing of veneers, other circumstances influenced the value of veneer and the need to improve veneer sawing. The advent of veneered furniture signaled a more capitalized furniture industry with a reliance on specialization and a concern for restricting the cost of materials while offering diverse products. In the early national period, furniture retailers, who were businessmen rather than craftsmen, began to control the low and middle segments of the market. They strove to keep a wide range of work on hand in their showrooms, but kept expenses under control by supplying the raw materials to individual pieceworkers who were not full-time employees. Veneered furniture was ideally suited for this method of manufacture: it allowed for more cost-effective use of materials; carcases or frames could be made up in large batches that could then be customized with veneering during assembly or finishing; and veneered furniture could be produced as piecework or by small garret shops specializing in a particular furniture form. Veneer could also cover frames or carcases of varying construction or quality.[10]

To meet the demands of the growing number of retail showrooms and warehouses, the ingenious rural craftsmen found ways to be more productive: they used water power to saw boards and turn chair and leg parts, women and children wove rush seats for chairs, and skilled painters and stainers used inlaid stringing to give maple and birch chairs the appearance of rosewood, and chests and case furniture the appearance of mahogany. These rural furnituremakers helped to develop widening markets during the first half of the

nineteenth century, but soon lost their position due to the advent of the railroad and the spread of the industry across the Midwest.[11]

While veneered furniture retained its viability during much of the first half of the nineteenth century, westward expansion and changing trade patterns affected wood choices and wood use. With the settlement of the upper Midwest came the increased availability of black walnut, an ideal wood for cabinetmaking. Cincinnati, Ohio, Chicago, Illinois, and Grand Rapids, Michigan, became the centers of middle-class furniture production. The scale of their production, easy access to the walnut stands, and the ease of shipping goods by railroad eroded the local monopolies of the rural centers in New England and elsewhere. Urban shops in the East retained some of their position, but often concentrated on the upper end of the market. By the middle of the century, eastern shops were importing walnut from the Midwest, mahogany from Central America, or rosewood from Brazil.[12]

The resurgence of oak as a common material at the end of the nineteenth century has traditionally been linked to the Arts and Crafts reformers' call for honest, indigenous materials. It can also be explained, however, by the depletion of the supply of walnut from midwestern forests. Until the 1890s, most designers and cabinetmakers disliked oak as a primary wood. They faulted its coarse, open grain and its yellowish tone when finished with varnish. As walnut became more scarce and more expensive in the last decade of the century, David Kendall of Grand Rapids pioneered the development of dark finishes that took the curse out of oak and made it more compatible with darker woods, such as walnut and mahogany. The increased possibilities for oak then led to widespread cutting of the previously neglected first-growth oaks.

Card table, probably Boston, Massachusetts (1790-1820). Mahogany, eastern white pine, mahogany and satinwood veneers. (H: 29^{1}/$_{4}$ in., W: 36 in., D: 17^{1}/$_{8}$ in.)

Card tables of identical shape and similar veneers were made by Elisha Tucker of Boston and retailed by William Leverett. Emery Moulton of Lynn and Jacob Sanderson of Salem also made very similar tables, indicating the possibility of widespread subcontracting within Massachusetts. (Yale University Art Gallery, The Mabel Brady Garvan Collection [1930.2597].)

Their great size made them ideal for the quarter-sawing that produced the attractive ray fleck of Mission furniture. The furniture industry's use of wood that was cheap and available was simply made more popular through the Arts and Crafts Movement's emphasis on native, traditional materials.[13]

In the 1910s, as the supply of large trees declined and the demand for colonial revival furnishings expanded, oak lost its prominence. The furniture industry began to harvest woods in the South, primarily gum (*Liquidambar styraciflua* or *Nyssa sylvatica*), yellow poplar, oak, birch, and maple. The great variety of stains developed during this period permitted the use of these woods for exteriors as well as interiors. Walnut, cherry, imported American mahogany (*Swietenia* spp.), African mahogany (*Khaya* spp.), and Philippine lauan (*Shorea* spp.) were also popular primary woods.[14]

At the high end of the market, the work of the Jacques Emile Ruhlmann and other *ensembliers* of the early twentieth century relied upon the colonial exploitation of wood resources. The availability of richly figured wood from Southeast Asia and Africa, areas being newly opened to commercial logging, played an essential role in the appearance of the Moderne work of the 1920s. Designs by Donald Deskey, Eugene Schoen, and Paul Frankl made extensive use of Macassar ebony (*Diospyros* spp.), bubinga (*Guibourtia* spp.), zebrawood (*Microberlinia brazzavillensis*), and other tropical woods. Previously, ebony had been so expensive that, in the 1870s and 1880s, even the leading custom-furniture firms, such as Herter Brothers, used ebonized cherry rather than real ebony. Likewise, in the nineteenth century, the Hawaiian wood koa (*Acacia koa*), long considered hard to work and used only out of necessity, was rarely exported. By the twentieth century, however, modern machinery had made it more workable, and its figure and color, similar to mahogany, made it more desirable.[15]

The reliance on figured tropical woods in solid and veneer form has continued throughout this century, suggesting that timber brokers in the tropics have played a large role in the fashion for woods. The mahogany industry grew rapidly during World War II, when it provided American and African mahogany for the construction of PT boats, gliders, and airplanes. After the war, it sought new markets. The industry stressed the suitability of mahogany as the perfect furniture wood due to its strength-to-weight ratio and its ease of working. It was also promoted as the perfect architectural wood, due to the great size of its boards and the evenness of the grain. The importers emphasized that mahogany could even be stained to match the light woods of the Scandinavian Modern work then popular. Much of the modern furniture industry followed the advice of the mahogany promoters.[16]

In the 1950s, designers such as Paul McCobb and woodworkers such as Wharton Esherick and Sam Maloof chose to work in domestic hardwoods. They embraced the commonness, warmth, and local availability of woods such as maple, cherry, and walnut, as well as the opportunity to work solid material. Esherick commented, "If I can't make something beautiful out of what's in my backyard, I'd better not make anything." Maloof preferred common walnut, replete with knots and sapwood, in order to highlight the organic quality of his elements and shaping.[17]

The emphasis on materials by this first generation of studio furnituremakers led to an obsession with a wider variety of species. George Nakashima, in particular, collected richly figured woods from throughout the world and explored the "soul" of each board. In the 1970s, many second-generation studio furnituremakers emphasized the color and grain of various exotics, such as purpleheart (*Pettogyne* spp.), bubinga, pau amarello (*Euxylophora paraensis*), teak (*Tectona grandis*), rosewood, padauk (*Pterocarpus* spp.), bloodwood (*Brosimum paraense*), and wenge (*Millettia* spp.). The interest in mixed media and painted surfaces in the 1980s checked this expansion and escalation of tropical timber use.[18]

Sideboard, made by Gustav Stickley's Craftsman Workshops, Eastwood, New York (1909-1912). White oak, chestnut, birch, oak veneer, oak plywood. (H: 47³/₄ in., W: 56¹/₈ in., D: 21¹/₄ in.)

Through his Craftsman Workshops and *Craftsman* magazine, Gustav Stickley popularized the use of fumed, quarter-sawn oak on modern Mission-style furniture. This sideboard features the rectilinear lines, hammered metal hardware, and figured oak that were characteristic of his designs. The richly figured doors are covered in quarter-sawn, white-oak veneer. (Yale University Art Gallery, gift of Dr. and Mrs. Matthew Newman [1979.27].)

Analysis of wood choices reveals that, throughout history, materials have not been chosen simply as a consequence of changing aesthetic fashion. Rather, design, materials, and furniture production are inextricably linked to a complex web of social, cultural, and economic factors, and it is appropriate that this catalogue and exhibition initiate new perspectives on the ecological history of furnituremaking. ⚓

Endnotes

1. For English examples, see Robert W. Symonds and Thomas Ormsbee, *Antique Furniture of the Walnut Period* (New York: Robert M. McBride & Co., 1947); Victor Chinnery, *Oak Furniture, The British Tradition* (Woodbridge: Antique Collectors' Club, 1980); Ralph Edwards, *The Dictionary of English Furniture from the Middle Ages to the Late Georgian Period* (1954. Reprint. Woodbridge: Antique Collectors' Club, 1983); and Geoffrey Wills, *English Furniture 1550-1760* (New York: Doubleday, 1971). For the American view, see Herbert Cescinsky and George Leland Hunter, *English and American Furniture* (Grand Rapids, Michigan: The Dean-Hicks Company, 1929); and Charles Nagel, *American Furniture 1650-1850* (New York: Chanticleer Press, 1949).

2. The path-breaking American furniture historians who pioneered the use of wood identification include Joseph Downs, *American Furniture: Queen Anne and Chippendale Periods* (New York: Bonanza Books, 1952), and Charles Montgomery, *American Furniture: The Federal Period* (New York: Viking Press, 1966). Some more recent scholars have explored the working properties and appropriate use of species: Benno Forman, *American Seating Furniture 1630-1730* (New York: W.W. Norton, 1988), pp. 19-38; and Philip Zea, "Construction Methods and Materials," in Brock Jobe and Myrna Kaye, *New England Furniture: The Colonial Era* (Boston: Houghton Mifflin, 1984), pp. 73-100.

3. For a broad-based approach to design, see Adrian Forty, *Objects of Desire* (New York: Pantheon, 1985).

4. For the best summary of seventeenth-century joinery, see Robert Trent, "New England Joinery and Turning Before 1700," in Robert Trent and Jonathan Fairbanks, eds., *New England Begins: The Seventeenth Century* (Boston: Museum of Fine Arts, Boston, 1982), pp. 501-510, and the catalogue entries that follow. On the English view of wood resources, in contrast to the Native American, see William Cronon, *Changes in the Land: Indians, Colonists, and the Ecology of New England* (New York: Hill and Wang, 1983), especially pp. 108-126.

5. See Bernard Bailyn, *New England Merchants in the Seventeenth Century* (New York: Harper Row, 1964); Barbara Ward, "The Craftsman in a Changing Society: Boston Goldsmiths, 1690-1730,"

(PhD dissertation, Boston University, 1983), especially pp. 157-244; Abbott Lowell Cummings, "Beginnings of Provincial Architecture in Boston, 1690-1725," *The Journal of the Society of Architectural Historians* 42 (March 1983), pp. 43-53; Trent, pp. 522-24 and 536-38; and Gerald W.R. Ward, *American Case Furniture in the Mabel Brady Garvan and Other Collections at Yale University* (New Haven: Yale University Art Gallery, 1988), pp. 125-28.

6. See Benno Forman, "Urban Aspects of Massachusetts Furniture in the Late Seventeenth Century," in John Morse, ed., *Country Cabinetwork and Simple City Furniture* (Charlottesville: University Press of Virginia, 1970), pp. 1-33; Edward S. Cooke, Jr., "The Warland Chest: Early Georgian Furniture in Boston," *Maine Antique Digest* (March 1987), section C, pp. 10-13; and Jobe and Kaye.

7. The discussion of Boston work from this period is drawn from Jobe and Kaye; and Wallace Gusler, "Variations in 18th-Century Casework: Some 'Old Masters' Built Better than Others," *Fine Woodworking* 23 (July 1980), pp. 50-53. Gary Nash's *The Urban Crucible* (Cambridge: Harvard University Press, 1979) provides valuable insight into changing economic relationships between New England and the Middle Colonies.

8. On Newport, see Michael Moses, *Master Craftsmen of Newport: The Townsends and Goddards* (Tenafly, New Jersey: MMI Americana Press, 1984); Jeanne Vibert Sloane, "John Cahoone and the Newport Furniture Industry," *Old-Time New England* 72 (1987), pp. 88-122; and Margaretta Lovell, "'Such Furniture as Will Be Most Profitable': The Business of Cabinetmaking in Eighteenth-Century Newport," *Winterthur Portfolio* 26, no. 1 (Spring 1991), pp. 27-62.

9. On the operation of local networks, see Edward S. Cooke, Jr., *Social Economy in Preindustrial America: The Woodworkers of Newtown and Woodbury, Connecticut, 1760-1820* (Baltimore: Johns Hopkins University Press, forthcoming); and William Hosley and Gerald Ward, eds., *The Great River: Art & Society of the Connecticut River Valley, 1635-1820* (Hartford: Wadsworth Atheneum, 1985).

10. The advantages of veneered work in decentralized production is discussed by Forty, pp. 55-59. On the American trade during this period, the most insightful work is Benjamin Hewitt, *The Work of Many Hands: Card Tables in Federal America, 1790-1820* (New Haven: Yale University Art Gallery, 1982).

11. John Tarrent Kenney, *The Hitchcock Chair* (New York: Clarkson Potter, Inc., 1971); Edwin Churchill, *Simple Forms and Vivid Colors* (Augusta: Maine State Museum, 1983).

12. On the mid-nineteenth century, see Donald Peirce, "Mitchell and Rammelsberg: Cincinnati Furniture Manufacturers, 1847-1881," *Winterthur Portfolio* 13, pp. 209-29; Sharon Darling, *Chicago Furniture: Art, Craft, & Industry, 1833-1983* (New York: W.W. Norton, 1984); and Ken Ames, "Grand Rapids Furniture at the Time of the Centennial," *Winterthur Portfolio* 10 (1975), pp. 23-50.

13. See Don Marek, *Arts and Crafts Furniture Design: The Grand Rapids Connection 1895-1915* (Grand Rapids, Michigan: Grand Rapids Art Museum, 1987), especially pp. 29-30 and 49; and "Robert Edwards, the Art of Work," in Wendy Kaplan, ed., *"The Art That is Life": The Arts & Crafts Movement in America, 1875-1920* (Boston: Museum of Fine Arts, Boston, 1987), pp. 223-36.

14. U.S. Department of Commerce, *Furniture: Its Selection and Use* (Washington: Government Printing Office, 1931), especially 21-33; and Darling, pp. 50-51.

15. On the work of the 1920s, see Karen Davies, *At Home in Manhattan: Modern Decorative Arts, 1925 to the Depression* (New Haven: Yale University Art Gallery, 1983); A.U. Chastain-Chapman, "Jacques-Emile Ruhlmann," and Nick Monjardo and David Parson, "Restoring Ruhlmann," *Fine Woodworking* 51 (March/April 1985), pp. 30-37. On the popularity of koa, see Irving Jenkins, *Hawaiian Furniture and Hawaii's Cabinetmakers, 1820-1940* (Honolulu: Editions Limited for The Daughters of Hawaii, 1983).

16. George Lamb, *The Mahogany Book* (Chicago: The Mahogany Association, 1946).

17. On the use of local woods among early studio furnituremakers, see Michael Stone, *Contemporary American Woodworkers* (Salt Lake City, Utah: Peregrine Smith, 1985); and Edward S. Cooke, Jr., "Clarity & Perfectibility: The Work of Sam Maloof," *Catalogue of the Philadelphia Craft Show* (1991), pp. 8-12.

18. On the woods of the 1970s to the present, see Edward S. Cooke, Jr., *New American Furniture: The Second Generation of Studio Furnituremakers* (Boston: Museum of Fine Arts, Boston, 1989).

Desk, designed by Donald Deskey, made by Schmied, Hungate and Kotzian, New York (1929). Yellow poplar, mahogany, chestnut, ash, Macassar ebony veneer, plywood, brass. (H: 41⅞ in., W: 48⅛ in., D: 21⅝ in.)

To get the most out of a precious exotic wood, the makers veneered Macassar ebony to a yellow poplar carcase. (Yale University Art Gallery, gift of Mrs. Arthur D. Berliss, Sr. [1984.23.2].)

Design for a Sustainable World
The Hooke Park experience

John Makepeace

Trees are the world's most energy-efficient and renewable source of structural material. Yet, for two centuries, industry has increasingly exploited minerals, such as coal, oil, and iron ore, using high-energy processes to create "new" materials. This exploitation of nonrenewable resources has led to ever-increasing waste and environmental damage. At the same time, original native forests—both temperate and tropical—are raped of their best trees, the source of the finest seed removed without regard for the long-term regeneration of distinctive species of superb genetic quality, which have adapted over eons to local soils and climates. Extensive areas of the world, once densely forested, have been cleared to fuel industrial and domestic needs, exposing soils that are incapable of supporting previously self-reliant communities.

Trees conserve and convert the earth's primary source of energy—the sun—into structural material. Minimal further energy is required to turn them into building components and products. Local timber processing requires relatively low capital investment and causes minimal pollution. Nontoxic preservatives can extend

(left) Hooke Park College is situated on 350 acres of broadleaf and conifer woodland in Dorset, England. The rich diversity of species provides an abundant source of local materials for construction of the school's buildings, as well as the design and production of innovative, ecological products. (Photo courtesy of The Parnham Trust.)

(above) A site of special interest to Hooke Park College for its rich diversity of native species: beech, alder, and hazel coppice. (Photo courtesy of The Parnham Trust.)

the life and utility of these native materials without resorting to energy-intensive pressure treatment, which weakens timber by fifteen percent. Well-managed woodlands foster a diversity of flora and fauna and stimulate the quality and productivity of the standing timber crop, generating a broad range of other social and environmental advantages.

Today, through scientific research and developments in technology, the world's surpluses of labor and land have the potential to provide renewable resources for the future. Conflict rages, however, between the extremes of commercial exploitation and ardent conservation. Despite the benefits of scientific scholarship, industrialists and policymakers in the United States, Australia, South America, and the Far East seem oblivious to the errors of those earlier cultures in the Middle East, Africa, and Europe, who cleared their own forests. Conversely, the conservation lobby too often forgets the remarkable capacity of nature to renew itself. Not only does cropping stimulate growth, but intelligent cropping stimulates quality.

The coppice industries, still found today in Britain and France, and the French oak forests both contain valuable lessons for a world facing timber shortages. Utilizing short timber rotations of naturally renewable forest crops, Europe's coppice industries supplied a host of small-diameter material for buildings, roads, vehicles, industrial components, furniture, and fuel. The regular income generated by such activities made it possible to allow prime trees to grow to maturity to provide seed as well as major timbers for ships, housing, and civil-engineering projects. Shortages of construction timber became acute during the eighteenth century, and the deficiency was met by imports. The manufacture of cottage furniture was located in the forest, but the availability of luxurious timbers from the New World, associated with the fashion for the exotic, led to the establishment of more efficient production operations—first at the ports of entry, and later at the main population centers. As the traditional craft techniques dwindled, so did the relationship between the growing of high-quality indigenous woods and the essential corollary of local markets and manufacturing.

In the eighteenth century, timber shortages prompted France to introduce quality-oriented forest policies. As a result of farsighted government intervention, the great oak forests of France, established under Napoleon, flourished, due to careful genetic selection and management based on sound scientific research. They have since become a part of the French culture and a unique industrial asset.

Today, the lack of clear and consistent national and international forestry policies leaves many designers either ignorant or just confused. Our culture is characterized by a serious rift in its relationship with nature. The individual has increasingly become a consumer of the environment, unable to distinguish between life-promoting and life-threatening thoughts and actions, torn between the ideals of technology and ecology.

Herein lies the challenge. Technology makes things possible, but unfettered technology leads to self-destruction. Through scientific research, education, and innovation, technology can be directed according to the laws of nature. Together, technology and ecology offer the enormously exciting prospect of a healthier and sustainable world. With this end in mind, The Parnham Trust of Dorset, England, through Hooke Park College, is pioneering a multi-disciplinary approach to forestry, industry, design, and education.

Early in my career as a designer and furnituremaker, a series of discoveries made me appreciate the blinkered effect of specialized education. It was commonly believed that "artistic" people were unlikely to succeed at business or in other practical matters. This notion seemed absurd and prompted me to action. I purchased historic Parnham House in 1976 to provide larger studios for my work, a place for public showings, as well as a center for a residential college.

Parnham House's first goal was to provide a coordinated education in design, furnituremaking, and business management for talented and highly motivated individuals. From my study of woodland management and its byproducts, I began to recognize the need for a more integrated industrial and environmental education. This led to The Parnham Trust's purchase in 1983 of a 350-acre forest, four miles from Parnham, which provided a superb location for Hooke Park College, founded in 1989.

A subsidiary of The Parnham Trust, Hooke Park offers a practical postgraduate program in forest-product technology. Accredited by Bournemouth University in Dorset, the program prepares students to set up businesses on an industrial scale to produce quality products for a wide market.

The college's goals are to teach students how to:

— employ neglected and renewable natural resources (people, land, and trees) in design and manufacturing enterprises

— develop affordable products and buildings made from timber

— maximize the use of forest products through a closer integration of manufacturing and timber production

The training workshops for Hooke Park College comprise three vaulted modules, made from locally harvested spruce thinnings. The thinnings are bent and joined to form an arch and are braced laterally to form a shell. (Photo courtesy of The Parnham Trust.)

— stimulate the planting and management of high-quality trees for their social and economic value

— work as entrepreneurs in ecological design, marketing, production, and business administration

Hooke Park College has brought together an international team of foresters, chemists, engineers, designers, and technicians to identify and find ways to overcome the traditional obstacles to efficient use of forest products in building design and construction—including the construction of the college's own training and residential facilities. (In 1993, the first buildings received an American Institute of Architects award in the category of sustainable communities.)

The physical structure of Hooke Park College demonstrates principles of ecologically sound design and technology. Small-diameter forest thinnings of spruce (*Picea* spp.) are culled from young plantations to favor the growth of superior trees. The thinnings, which have no commercial value, are kept in the round, treated with preservatives, and employed for all the structural components of the college buildings. These thinnings form the structural matrix of the lattice-shell roof of the college's Training Centre, shown on p. 30, where they gain great strength in compression.

Buildings of all kinds are responsible for half of all energy consumed in the world, and the associated production of carbon dioxide is the major contributor to global warming. Other climatic factors, such as damage to the ozone layer by chlorofluorocarbons (CFCs) and forest depletion are also associated with the construction, contents, and use of buildings. Hooke Park's next challenge will be to develop student and staff housing that will demonstrate greater energy efficiency in both construction and operation. Research into the efficient recycling of heat and water and the composting of organic waste will be combined with the development of cost-effective building systems to meet a variety of housing needs.

A significant number of the graduates of Hooke Park College come to the school with a degree in architecture or design or have a background in professional woodworking. Through the program, they come to understand the combined principles of forestry,

conservation, marketing, manufacturing, and business management. A rich variety of innovative products, designed and executed by graduates, is already on the market in Great Britain. Andy Simmonds offers an ecological design and building service in Buckinghamshire. Malcolm Strong designs and builds bridges in sensitive landscapes for Scottish National Heritage. Richard Eccleston and Nigel Prestwich combine a portable sawmilling service with the design and construction of garden structures, such as gazebos, balustrades, pergolas, and porticos. John Russell Saunders makes spruce and ash (*Fraxinus* spp.) furniture sold by The Victoria and Albert Museum in London. Richard Foyle and Roy Tam (a contributor to this exhibition) design and manufacture high-grade contract and domestic furniture from ash thinnings. Petter Southall combines green-wood and boatbuilding techniques

(above) Study Chair, ash, designed and built by Trannon Furniture Ltd. (Photo by Roy Tam, courtesy of The Parnham Trust.)

(right) Ark Bowls, ash, built by James Marston in various sizes. (Photo courtesy of Hooke Park College.)

in distinctive and stylish furniture, and Jim Marston bends and rivets ash laths into bowls and baskets for a wide retail market.

The scope is boundless. As a result of this program, these students, and others like them, are challenging many of the traditional conventions of timber construction and developing fresh solutions, more appropriate to changing circumstances.

Many designer-makers, as well as others, isolate themselves through specialization. Their work, therefore, risks becoming egocentric. Often they feel that the scale and influence of their effort is so limited in comparison to that of industry that they have no reason to consider the issues raised by this exhibition.

To the contrary, I believe that artists play a leading role in a consumer society. With the extraordinary liberty they enjoy comes an inescapable responsibility. The values they express through their work can either provide inspiration for environmental development or can promote further disregard for and destruction of the natural world. Through their intimate involvement with materials, methods, and messages, artists and designers have a unique opportunity to influence public opinion.

Young people are sensitive to the issues. It falls to designers to lead and to educators to promote a more profound understanding of the relationship between ecology, technology, and design. ⬆

Responsible Woodworking
A personal odyssey

Silas Kopf

Some time around 1980 an article was published in a science magazine describing the fragility of tropical forest ecosystems. The scenario was something like this: population pressures force people into previously uninhabited forests; trees are cut to clear land for agriculture; the land proves to be less fertile than it initially appeared, and agriculture can't be sustained; the land is abandoned and new land is cleared; the old land bakes in the tropical sun and is then severely eroded during the rainy season, leaving territory that will never again be capable of supporting a rich forest. The cycle continues.

Although the article was disturbing, I took solace in the fact that it didn't point the finger at my profession. Sad as this series of events might be, the author allowed as how greed for wood was not the cause of the problem. I didn't have any complicity through my use of tropical wood. Or did I?

My work focuses on marquetry and the use of a wide variety of colors and species of wood to produce the desired effects. I *need*

Marquetry detail from an ebony cabinet attributed to André Charles Boulle (1642-1732), cabinetmaker for Louis XIV. The panel is made of various woods on a tortolseshell background. (In the collection of the Musée du Louvre. Photo courtesy of Musees Nationaux, Paris, France.)

to use exotic tropical woods, and the implications of giving them up were too disturbing to contemplate. In fact, my career depended on a continued supply of these woods. But the depletion of the rainforests was becoming equally hard to ignore, as it obviously threatened my supply of materials.

Furniture and woodcraft has made significant use of exotic wood since the sixteenth century. The great cabinetmakers of France were called *ébénistes* (workers of ebony). Could we eventually find ourselves without ebony (*Diospyros* spp.) to use? The great English furniture of the Chippendale period used Cuban mahogany (*Swietenia mahagoni*) and, through overexploitation, this wood is no longer available.

I watched as it became unconscionable to use another exotic material in craft and furniture. Ivory has decorated furniture since the time of ancient Egypt, but in the 1980s we had finally reduced the elephant population to the point that it might never again support a viable commercial ivory trade. Could the overexploitation of Brazilian rosewood (*Dalbergia nigra*) or satinwood (*Chloroxylon swietenia*) reach the same crisis? Some might say it already has!

In 1980 I wasn't aware of a reactionary movement, but I could imagine that people might someday avoid furniture that incorporated exotic woods, much as they had begun to avoid ivory jewelry and fur coats. To a maker of marquetry furniture, this was troubling. And even if I were not affected immediately, it was sad to think that my daughter's generation might not be able to make furniture with marquetry decoration because the opportunity had been squandered in my lifetime.

Some suggested, even then, that the proper thing to do was to boycott tropical woods. While this might be a workable solution for some, I found there to be a qualitative difference between our temperate hardwoods and some exotic species. Many tropical timbers are seductively beautiful, and, for centuries, consumers have demonstrated their interest. Forcing the craftsman to choose cherry (*Prunus* spp.) instead of bubinga (*Guibourtia* spp.) seemed unfair—not to mention the hardship a boycott might cause for producing countries. There had to be a middle ground.

Eventually, I came to understand that logging plays a crucial role in the loss of rainforests. The roads made by timber companies open vast areas of virgin forest to further exploitation and settlement. Timber and reforestation programs are either nonexistent or ineffective. Forest destruction would abate only if mature trees were selectively cut and small trees were left to grow. Selective cutting might also leave a suitable animal habitat and an environment that could support a variety of plant life. But selective logging is more expensive than clearcutting. Where would the money come from? Could I afford to pay more for my material if it came from a well-managed source? Clearly, today's market does not account for the exploitation of the environment. Brazilian mahogany (*Swietenia macrophylla*) is cheaper than a low-grade walnut (*Juglans* spp.) grown in my own backyard.

Most custom furnituremakers build luxury objects, or at least objects of significant expense. Most of our cost is in labor. Couldn't the customers for our products absorb a substantially higher material expense?

I decided to try to educate my customers, as I had been educated myself, about the true costs of conservation and the justification for paying more. But the problem, I quickly discovered, was that there were no ready sources of wood from "sustainably" managed forests. These were yet to be developed. In the interim, I decided to attach an "ecology surtax." I added the dollar value of the tropical woods used in the piece to the final price, to make the point that the true cost of my materials would have been significantly higher if the market were to account for the cost of conservation. I donated the money raised through this surcharge to a nonprofit organization working to protect rainforests. The surtax had the added benefit of involving my clients directly in the decision of whether or not to use exotic woods. They could then ask about the alternatives and, in the process, come to a better understanding of the issues.

I am often asked why I concern myself with this issue when I use so little wood. While it is true that the amount of exotic wood used by all the custom woodworkers in the United States is probably so small as to not make a tangible impact on deforestation worldwide, I like to think of myself as casting a vote. My choosing to recycle may not affect the landfill, but if everyone recycles, it will certainly make a difference. In the same way, woodworkers can have an impact on forest management if they speak with a united voice and through their buying patterns. "High-end" design can also have a ripple effect in industry that—for better or for worse—can lead to a wider interest in certain woods or wood treatments. Until they realize that consumers and manufacturers want to limit their complicity in the thoughtless destruction of our forest resources, suppliers won't look for alternatives.

I suspect that the dynamics are similar to those at work in the organic-produce market. Until enough people demanded pesticide-free carrots from their grocers, these vegetables didn't find their way to market. After many years of grassroots effort, consumers are beginning to have a choice in the way they buy wood. This "good wood" market is in its infancy, but I am confident that it will continue to grow as the crisis intensifies.

Apart from choosing our materials more carefully, what else can woodworkers do to demonstrate our respect for the precious timber resources upon which our livelihood depends? We can be more thoughtful about the way we use all wood and, when we can, use veneer of exotic materials to get the most out of them. We can be more scrupulous in our designs in order to conserve material and we can build objects to the best of our ability so that they will last for generations of use. It is no exaggeration to say that entire civilizations have been built upon the use of wood. It is not too late to reexamine our relationship with trees and the forest. Not yet. ⚲

Ecological Design in Industry

Four companies lead the way

Seth Stem

*D*uring the last few years, a number of industries have begun to address the issue of sustaining the world's wood resources. The motivating factors are linked to society's growing conservation consciousness. Environmental groups and the media have spotlighted a variety of ecological concerns—from oil spills to the impending demise of the spotted owl and other species to the destruction of the rainforest. This increasing awareness has translated into pressure from consumers, which has affected industry's profits both positively and negatively.

Wood products manufactured with seemingly politically correct practices can mean increased profits. Using a lesser-known but available species of wood may not only reduce material costs, but also improve the product's public image. Businesses have begun using conservation issues as marketing tools, and some companies design entire product lines around wood from sustainable sources. Unfortunately, others simply use catch phrases to make their existing products look good to an ecologically aware market. (Advertisement stabs such as "This cutting board uses no rainforest woods" do not necessarily mean that the woods come from a well-managed source.)

On the other hand, government regulations now require that American businesses spend huge sums of money to meet new pollution standards. In many cases these controls have made competition in the global marketplace more difficult, so some companies have developed the mindset that improving the environment negatively affects profit margins. While it's unlikely that these companies will apply pressure for correct conservation practices, the potential imposition of even more stringent government regulations may eventually motivate them to give more consideration to their wood sources.

One incontrovertible reason for manufacturers of wood products to address conservation issues is to ensure that there is material for their own future use. Industry regards the availability of many wood species as endless. In fact, one may still purchase huge quantities of mahogany (*Swietenia* spp.), as well as many North American hardwoods. Although these commonly used wood species will probably be available for some time to come, their dimensions are getting smaller and the price is increasing. The short-sighted may choose to ignore this problem, but it will not go away.

The role of the designer in the pattern of material use is important. In their product specifications, designers, especially the new generation of industrial designers, have begun to take into account the environmental impact of the use of materials, whether plastic, metal, or wood. Designers now consider whether the use of a material will be perceived as a positive or negative factor in the public acceptance of the product. They want to know if the material they are recommending is a sustainable resource or if it is going to harm the environment at any stage of its development, manufacture, or disposal.

In this life-cycle assessment of a material, the designer evaluates all aspects of the potential environmental impact of the product throughout its lifespan: how much energy is used, or damage done to the environment, or pollution created in producing or harvesting the raw material and transporting it to the point of manufacture? What waste materials and types of pollution are produced, how much energy is consumed, and what potential health hazards to factory workers are presented in the manufacturing processes? The issue of quality—the longevity of the product in relationship to total resources used and environmental impact—are examined. A product with a potential life span of twenty years is more justifiable in terms of resources consumed than a similar product that uses the same resources, but is expected to last only ten years. Disposal factors are also considered: is the whole product recyclable or are any of its easily separated components? Are the materials biodegradable? What kinds of pollution result from the recycling or destruction of the product?

Today, the industrial designer must research and consider an entirely new level of information about materials—beyond their aesthetic and performance values and standard properties. Well-respected educational institutions, such as Rhode Island School of Design (RISD) and others, must be committed to making these practices part of the industrial designer's training. RISD offers a course entitled "Ecological Responsibilities of Artists and Designers," which addresses as design issues environmental ethics, recycling, and the sources of materials. The Industrial Design Department also integrates these issues into its studios and has worked within the industry as well as entered design competitions that focus on recyclable materials. This exhibition and catalogue are the most recent manifestation of RISD's concerns.

Several companies have also considered these issues and have made commendable efforts to design new products or revise existing ones for the sake of intelligent wood use. Notable among them are The Martin Guitar Company, The Knoll Group, Portico Door Company, and Bridge City Tool Works.

The Martin Guitar Company in Nazareth, Pennsylvania, has traditionally manufactured some of the world's finest acoustic instruments from woods such as rosewood (*Dalbergia nigra*), mahogany, and spruce (*Picea* spp.)—woods that have been found over the centuries to have the right properties for instrument making. Sitka spruce (*Picea sitchensis*) is one of the tone woods preferred for soundboards, and Martin Guitar has discovered a bountiful alternative source of old-growth Sitka spruce logs, reclaiming wood from abandoned Alaskan salmon traps. During the past year, Martin Guitar has made a directed effort to develop alternatives to endangered species of rainforest woods, seeking instead to use domestic hardwoods, such as cherry (*Pinus* spp.), walnut (*Juglans* spp.), maple (*Acer* spp.), ash (*Fraxinus* spp.), basswood

(*Tilia* spp.), and mesquite (*Prosopis* spp.). This presented quite a design challenge, because the woods in a musical instrument are selected for a wide range of properties, including stability, density, tonality, and aesthetic quality. Martin Guitar evaluated these domestic species for their ability to produce tones that could be rated as "well balanced throughout, clear, sweet, good projection." Results ranged from such optimum ratings to "shallow bass, tinny treble, lacks projection." According to Dick Boak, director of advertising, walnut proved to be the best of the woods tested.

Michael Dresdner, of the research and development department, states in his synopsis of Martin's "sustainable-yield" design effort: "We decided to build several guitars using only woods harvested in the United States. The paradox of the local argument for sustainability is that America is not currently providing a very good role model for responsible forest management, and a simple boycott of tropical timbers does not address the economic reality of Third World countries. However, we felt that choosing local woods at least keeps the raw-material source close to home, where it can be tightly monitored and verified."

The Knoll Group, in New York City, one of the largest manufacturers of office furnishings in the United States, has fully addressed the design and fabrication of an environmentally sound product in the development of a new chair series designed by Frank Gehry, a California-based architect with an international reputation. Gehry's bentwood chairs are made of maple veneer laminates, cross-woven like a basket to obtain a strong, flexible structure with a minimum of material. As Gehry explained in a Knoll press release, "Knoll was relentless in evaluating every material and process related to the furniture. We utilized sustainable resources and applied clean technologies without sacrificing design." The maple was harvested exclusively from the Menominee forest in Wisconsin (see p. 67).

In this recent series of experimental instruments, The Martin Guitar Company substituted a range of commonly available, domestic woods, such as cherry, walnut, maple, ash, basswood, and mesquite, for the traditional Sitka spruce, rosewood, and mahogany. (Photo by Dean Powell.)

The Menominee, who control 234,000 acres of forest land on their reservation, have been noted for practicing sustainable-forestry methods for decades and have recently been awarded certification by Scientific Certification Systems (SCS), an environmental-assessment company based in California.

Knoll also developed a finishing system for the chairs in which the pieces were dipped into, not sprayed with, water-based finishes. This process resulted in a ninety-eight percent efficiency in the application of the finish and eliminated potentially harmful, airborne pollutants from the workplace.

Portico Door Company, of San José, Costa Rica, has perhaps developed the ultimate approach to wood conservation by purchasing and managing its own forests to provide sustainable yields of royal "mahogany" (*Karapa guyanenses*), the primary material in its fine-quality doors. Until 1987, Portico purchased logs for its sawmills in the open market. Because of the company's concern with the apparently accelerating rate of deforestation in Costa Rica, however, Portico purchased several thousand acres of land on which it achieves sustainable yields of the species and avoids logging operations that significantly disturb the rainforest ecosystem.

For seven years, Bridge City Tool Works in Portland, Oregon, made a series of precision marking and measuring woodworking tools from brass and Brazilian rosewood. As a conservation measure, the company conscientiously purchased as much of the rosewood as possible in the form of cutoffs and seconds from The Martin Guitar Company. Although, historically, rosewood has been used for fine tool handles, in 1991, Bridge City began using Juara wood, a material made of beech or maple laminates that have been impregnated with phenolic resin. Bridge City reasoned that, even

(facing page) The maple used in Frank Gehry's bentwood collection was harvested by the Menominee Indians of central Wisconsin, whose forestry operations are considered a model of good management. (The Gehry Collection, photo by Jay Ahrend, courtesy of The Knoll Group.)

(left) Portico's doors are manufactured in Costa Rica, using royal "mahogany" (*Karapa guyanenses*) from the company's own forests. Portico was recently certified as "State-of-the-Art Well-Managed" by Scientific Certification Systems. (Photo courtesy of Portico Door Company.)

though it had been recycling waste material from another manufacturing process, the company did not wish to have its product associated with the use of an endangered wood species. In Juara, Bridge City found a substitute material that is stable, hard, and has its own inherent beauty, with a color, luster, and sparkle every bit as attractive as rosewood. The company also discovered that Juara makes a more durable and accurate tool.

All of this is a start. Increasingly, material sustainability and the welfare of the environment are becoming the responsibilities of industry and those who design for industry. Conscientious wood use and conservation depend not only on an awareness of the issues, but also on the perception of the value of a species and of how design can support its use and the use of its alternatives in industry and craft. ▲

Since 1991, Bridge City's elegant marking and measuring tools have been made of dyed maple, birch, or beech veneers, impregnated with phenolic resin. This new, synthesized material, used to make these squares, is more stable and dense than the tropical rosewood it replaces. (Photo courtesy of Bridge City Tool Works, Inc.)

CONSERVATION WITH AN AXE

Timothy J. Synnott

Laura K. Snook

Roy Keene

Scott Landis

FLOOD   WolfRIVER

THE REAR CR
X 24. WAITING FOR

Personal Visions, Public Statements
Design and resource conservation

Robert O'Neal

This exhibition and catalogue attempt to reveal the vital relationship between design and conservation and to explore how, in partnership, the two might change the current separateness of man and nature into a cooperative relationship and create a closer spiritual connectedness between us and the earth.

Through its products, design can increase our awareness of this dynamic relationship. By using materials and ideas skillfully, the designer-craftsman can make evident the fragility and wonder of the natural world. A very sound case has been made for approaching conservation from a technical, scientific point of view. Approached through art and design, however, the idea of conservation is integrated into the emotional fiber of our consciousness through mystery, ambiguity, and ritual. Presenting conservation through valued man-made objects is the first step in the process of making us aware of our place in the ecology of the world.

To date, industry has viewed nature and its resources as limitless and self-renewing. The rainforest, however, belies this assumption. A startling metaphor for the world we live in, the rainforest looks lush and fertile, but is in fact very fragile. Another of industry's misperceptions is an emphasis on design that encourages consumption for its own sake rather than on design as a problem-solving tool.

Traditionally, designers have been taught to consider all the factors that might affect a given design problem. After the designer has evaluated these, he or she shapes a comprehensive solution. Ideally, this process balances and channels the needs of the client, the user, and the designer in the final product. Unfortunately, in practice, this traditional view of design is often subverted by the view of it as a tool to hyperstimulate the market. New designs are created to promote sales and consumption, not necessarily to improve the product materially.

It is difficult to discuss the production of objects that spiritually and meaningfully connect us to the natural world without sounding trite. In this market-driven world, the "green" concept has already become a commercially exploited cliché. Design for conservation requires a return to the original, or modernist's, intent—that is, to replace the superfluous with the essential. Modernism in design originated as a philosophical reaction against visual and ornamental excess, but has evolved into a practical opportunity for design to become a creative response to the ecological, social, economic, and moral changes that our time demands.

Outstanding design provides people with the enriching and valuable opportunity to experience a designer's ability to relate materials, technology, and aesthetics. In this process, design can emerge as a proactive discipline with a strong, positive impact when practiced at its highest level. Ours is a time of instability and sweeping change. It is a time full of hope and promise, a time of retrenchment and fear. Designers and craftsmen must play a responsible part in conserving the world's resources and promoting the well-being of its people, rather than becoming the tools of business for expanded consumption and larger profits.

Conservation is critical to global ecology, which is essential to the welfare of the human race. The global concept extends well beyond a specific regionalist or nationalist concern for conserving a limited range of materials within a geographically defined area. As a means of communication, design can expand our awareness of the critical need to conserve. Conservation by design—that is, designing and creating objects from materials from protected and well-managed resources—will, over time, help stimulate an increased global awareness and better management of those resources. The process of giving greater consideration to the materials used in making an object is pivotal in bridging the ever-widening gap that has developed between man and nature since the beginning of the Industrial Revolution.

Design and craft are not an end, but rather a means to an end. Many objects will have to be produced over an extended period of time to create a deeper sensibility and understanding of our connectedness and responsibility to the natural world. In this way, design and craft are processes of evolution, as well as paradigms for more comprehensive action. Like conservation, design is the conscious imposition of limits to create a desired end. Man has so damaged the environment that letting natural systems try to right themselves is no longer enough. We must implement a plan of progressive ecology in order to survive. Design, craft, and conservation must together help to recreate an ecological, social, and cultural environment that brings into balance the relationship between man and the finite natural resources still available. We have to reinvent and restructure our processes, which up to now have been taken for granted.

The cultural heritage of the Americas is based on the strong belief in mankind's spiritual partnership with nature. The model provided by Native Americans serves as a reminder that global survival depends upon the respect and care we extend to the physical world and to each other. If designed well enough, objects, spaces, furniture, and products can become spiritual symbols of the mutually nurturing relationship of man and nature, with the power to transform our global culture by fostering the idea of living in partnership.

Forests for Tomorrow
Managing for timber and long-term conservation

Timothy J. Synnott

All over the world, natural forests are being cleared, degraded, and converted to other uses—the boreal and temperate forests of Asia, Europe, and America; the dry, wet, and montane tropical forests; and the southern temperate forests of Chile, southern Africa, and New Zealand. Even where forests are increasing in area, as in western Europe, old-growth natural forests are declining. The causes are many and varied, and behind them are a variety of driving forces—you could call them economics and population pressure, or you could call them greed and poverty.

Historically, many forests have been used, modified, and tenaciously protected by their traditional inhabitants and owners, but many old, indigenous cultures have also cleared immense forest areas. Some of them, such as the Yanomami in Brazil, purposely caused small changes in composition and structure, which were sustained for centuries. Elsewhere, as in the Mayan empires, large areas were cleared for irrigated agriculture, but the forest returned when populations declined. Great forests were cleared by the ancient Greeks, as lamented by Herodotus and Plato, and in the mountains of the Middle East since the time of the Phoenicians. Many of these areas have remained deforested to this day.

This forest in Cap Esterias, Gabon, West Africa, shows the results of successful management and natural regeneration of an indigenous species. Okoumé (*Aucoumea klaineana*), the main timber tree harvested by the French for decades in Gabon, is also an active colonizer. (Photo by Timothy J. Synnott.)

Although deforestation is not new, in this century the pace has increased enormously.

The time has long passed when indigenous people were left alone to protect or clear their own forests as they saw fit, without outside interference. The time has also passed when the fate of the forests was left to government foresters or to rich or royal landowners. These groups, which once played a vital role in conservation and management, are today under strong commercial pressures, and often promote too much use and not enough conservation.

All this is well known. What is new is that wood producers, consumers, and distributors are discovering that the combined effect of their decisions can have a powerful impact on forest-management practices. More and more, governments and international organizations are under popular pressure to protect the forests and the interests of future generations. This essay is intended to provide some guidelines for wood users who are concerned about the future of all forests—temperate as well as tropical—and who don't want to contribute to forest destruction.

It may be hard to believe, but the technical elements of forest management are not especially difficult. Some ecologists and activists maintain that no one knows how to manage tropical forests, that no one has ever done it sustainably, and that we know practically nothing about tropical forests. Certainly, at present, very few tropical forests are being managed. Still, the techniques for producing a long-term yield of forest products, while minimizing damage and maintaining the natural forest habitat are not difficult to put into practice, as long as the yields are calculated and controlled within safe limits. Just as any peasant farmer can manage a farm, so any forester, or untrained forest inhabitant, can carry out basic forest management and conserve the forest while producing forest products, if the opportunity and resources are available.

Tropical forestry for long-term conservation and commercial production was started in the Indian subcontinent. Some forestry was begun before the end of the eighteenth century, but state forestry started in the 1840s when the government responded to pressure from a well-connected, nongovernment organization concerned about erosion and deforestation.

The first government foresters were trained in Germany and France in the European tradition. They sometimes found that forestry in the tropics was easier than in Europe, where regeneration often repeatedly fails after unexpected frosts, snow, storms, or droughts. At first, these European foresters controlled logging as a careful, delicate operation. They avoided severe impacts, as they had learned to do from experience in Europe. Much later, they found that many tropical forests can regenerate successfully, even after heavy logging, fires, hurricanes, or farming (as long as the fires, grazing, and farming are not continued).

New techniques were developed in many countries of Asia and Africa. In the early 1920s, Belize led the way in intensive-management systems for mahogany production. Later still, plantation techniques were developed for the tropics, with wide spacing and heavy thinning. These techniques gradually influenced conservative plantation practices in Europe, where for centuries foresters imitated natural regeneration with dense planting and many light thinnings.

As forest dwellers discovered centuries ago, a low rate of timber extraction can be sustained indefinitely, but forest management deals with more than just logging. The difficult part is to manage a forest (or farm or fishery) for maximum yield and profit, while also satisfying all the desirable social, legal, and environmental standards. The system is liable to collapse if the rate of extraction is too high, if environmental protection and benefits to local communities are too low, and if some of the participants—loggers or landless farmers—are out of control. Good forest management has many of the same elements as any other enterprise: it is not just the forest that must be managed, but the whole productive and administrative operation, including its financial, human, and natural resources.

There is no mysterious or fundamental difference between temperate and tropical forestry. Both are complex, with biological and technical difficulties. They have always influenced each other, and will continue to do so, and both require a sound management system. Beyond the basic similarities, however, there is a crucial difference between typical timber-production practices in temperate regions and those in the tropics.

Government and forest services in some of the United States, and certainly in much of western Europe, aim at long-term timber production and other benefits (environmental, ecological, social) and have substantial control over logging. People may disagree over these controls, and whether they adequately protect the public interest and the benefits and values of the forests, but, undeniably, most public and private forests in the United States and Europe are managed. In this respect, temperate forestry resembles agriculture.

The situation is different in the American tropics. The great majority of forest land legally belongs to the state, and all countries have a framework of regulations, laws, and forestry staff. Forestry regulations in the tropics are often stricter than in temperate regions and usually also apply to private and communal forests. In practice, however, these rules are hardly observed or enforced. The state issues permits for logging and collects taxes on some of the timber cut, but neither the logging nor the forests are organized to ensure long-term supplies of timber, let alone the long-term future of the forests. Some timber companies in the tropics are well-managed enterprises, but most tropical forests are not.

Logging in the tropics is often compared with mining, where resources are plundered with no intention of ensuring future supplies. Ocean fishing is a better comparison. An exploited mine has no future whatsoever, although fisheries can usually remain productive indefinitely. Likewise, a forest that has been logged, even carelessly, can usually yield another harvest later on. Many tropical forests, especially in West Africa and tropical America, continue to produce timber after having been selectively logged several times, although they will ultimately be degraded if heavy equipment is used for intensive, uncontrolled logging.

In both the fishing and logging industries, the public and the enlightened players agree that controls are needed—although they have trouble agreeing on what the controls should be or how to implement them.

In temperate regions, foresters focus their efforts on improving existing management by increasing efficiency, by fairer distribution of benefits, or by giving higher priority to other objectives, such as recreation or conservation. In the tropics, the front line of action is in trying to introduce management into unmanaged forests or to reactivate management where it has lapsed.

Progress is being made. In Mexico, Costa Rica, and Trinidad, well-established management is in operation in several forests, and there are many smaller or newer projects in these and other countries.

They all aim at environmental protection, biological conservation, and social benefits, as well as forest products. The Plan Piloto Forestal in Quintana Roo, Mexico, begun in 1983, has led to the communal management of about two million acres of communally owned forests (see p. 55). The Portico forests in Costa Rica are

This *Acacia abyssinica*, from the Napore Hills in northern Uganda, shows a high degree of dichotomous branching and is covered with ferns, orchids, and other epiphytes. Photographed in Kidepo National Park, a typical unmanaged park on the Sudan border. (Photo by Timothy J. Synnott.)

owned and managed by a private company to supply its own industry. In Trinidad, the state has owned and managed its Forests Reserves since the 1930s, with some highly successful silvicultural systems, and it issues logging permits to many small companies. All these management systems rely on natural regeneration, with very little planting. The total area of managed forests in tropical America is much less than one percent of the total forest area, but these examples show that successful management is possible under a wide variety of circumstances and for many different objectives.

The introduction of basic management into unmanaged forests and the improvement of existing management are reasonable and realistic short-term goals, with the long-term objectives of reducing the rate of clearance of tropical forests and increasing the range of benefits from remaining forests.

There are three basic elements to forest management: the setting of objectives (such as wood production, biodiversity conservation, watershed protection, recreation, etc.), with priorities and the flexibility to adapt to changing circumstances; a system for controlling what happens (including controls on harvesting, fires, farming, and theft), neither too weak nor too rigid; and a system for monitoring and recording harvests, growth rates, forest conditions, costs, work done, as well as for the typical stocktaking and record-keeping of a long-term management enterprise.

In managed forests, the technical elements are usually described in management plans, sometimes in great detail. These plans include descriptions of the environment, resources, and past experience. More important, they should give a clear statement and justification of the objectives and how they should best be achieved, including the calculations leading to the proposed rate of harvesting, and of how the work programs and controls will be implemented.

Harvesting programs should be spelled out in detail, in terms of volumes, areas, species, and sizes. The intensity and frequency of harvests must be in balance to avoid the damage of overcutting and to make good use of the resources. In simple forest management, after a forest has been logged once, the first areas logged should be ready for logging again. There is no fixed formula, but the heavier the initial logging, the longer the wait until the next. A light logging every twenty years, or a heavier logging every sixty years may both give good results. The choice depends on the ecological requirements of the preferred species, their growth rates, and the costs and environmental impacts of harvesting.

Long-term yields of timber in tropical forests are typically about one cubic meter per hectare per year (about fifteen cubic feet per acre) of large commercial logs, averaged over a whole forest. In all natural forests, yields may be higher in areas of favorable climate, and they can be increased by treatments such as thinning, and by using smaller sizes and more species.

Many techniques have been successfully applied to change the structure and composition of tropical forests to increase tree growth and the regeneration of valuable species. Like thinning, silvicultural treatments usually work by eliminating unwanted trees, providing more space for existing trees and new seedlings of preferred species. The planting of seedlings in lines in the logged forest, known as enrichment planting, can be very successful in increasing the stock of valuable species. All these elements of more intensive management are expensive investments, so their economics and biological impacts need studying before they are implemented.

One of the most profitable ways to increase yields from tropical forests, and another element of good management, is the improved utilization of the existing timbers: use of more of the lesser-known species, more intensive logging, and more efficient processing. Sometimes, local transport costs and limited markets do not allow more intensive production, but highly selective logging is often a lost opportunity. Larger areas must be logged to satisfy the markets, and the future management prospects for these high-graded forests are bleak. It is even more regrettable when the easy profits are not reinvested for continued production and employment. Forests that have lost all their best trees, with no current production or management, are the most likely to be cleared for farming. Even so, the production of only large logs of a few valuable species can be part of good management, especially where the physical impact of logging must be kept to a minimum for environmental reasons.

As in any enterprise, management must be flexible and guided by common sense and the best available information. Our idea of good management will change with time and with the development of new techniques and new priorities. For example, foresters now pay much more attention to social welfare and species conservation than they did a generation ago and are beginning to include the benefits of carbon storage among their objectives.

In most of the tropics, the first step must be to bring the rate of harvesting and forest clearance under control. This requires planning and management and, most of all, the willingness of the key players: loggers, forest owners, the timber industry, the government, and the farmers who need land or another way to make a living.

There are two reasons for optimism. One is that in purely technical terms basic management is not especially difficult to achieve. In the second half of the last century and the first half of this one, many tropical countries introduced controlled logging and brought their forests under management. This happened mainly in the Philippines and in the former British colonies of present-day India, Burma, Malaysia, Nigeria, Ghana, Uganda, Trinidad, and Belize. If it could be done in so many countries then, surely it can be done now.

Admittedly, it was made easier by the lower populations and smaller commercial pressures of those times, and by the heavy hand of colonial governments. Many of the management systems broke down due to rising demands for land, changing political systems, and expanding opportunities for profitable trade. Now, in tropical America, it is harder to introduce logging under strict controls from the start. There are too many social, political, administrative, and economic problems to be resolved—but so there are in all developments. The technical problems are not overwhelming.

The other cause for optimism is that most countries have laws and policies requiring that logging and settlement be controlled and forests brought under long-term management. Efforts to introduce or improve basic management support these policies.

It is often argued, with vehemence, that foreigners and foreign organizations have no right to interfere in how another country's resources are used. Of course, it is not acceptable for foreign groups to dictate how management must be carried out while threatening economic penalties if it is not. In the case of tropical forests, however, basic management is a cause that could unite many groups in support of national laws and policies.

It is a common myth that improvements in forest management can be brought about by an act of political will (most common among those who believe that banks, governments, and economic advisers actually control what happens). Today, all over the world, governments are discovering that even when they have the will and a package of techniques, environmental problems remain intractable; there may be a lack of resources or too many vested interests or related social and economic problems. It is relatively easy, and perhaps temporarily satisfying, to organize aggressive campaigns of pressure on these governments, but it is not always the best use of energy and resources. Even when a government is serious about improving resource management, its priorities are not necessarily identical to those of foreign or national activists. For example, suggestions that eliminate existing jobs in the interest of environmental conservation are not met with enthusiasm in the tropics or in the Pacific Northwest.

There is always room for improvements and always some people trying to make them. If, within the existing constraints of resources, vested interests, and local problems, concerned parties can find these opportunities, they can play a constructive part.

The challenge for woodworkers, architects, and designers is to find a way of exerting their special influences. These groups are not well placed to operate through sanctions, bans, punitive tariffs, or military solutions—all of which have been suggested. I suggest that they also go beyond the publicity campaigns, public education, and fundraising enthusiastically pursued by many organizations.

The question is, How can regular wood buyers use their buying power as a force for promoting forest management?

Discussions about selective buying are taking place all over the world, among foresters, loggers, sawmillers, importers, and

High-impact, heavy-equipment logging, as practiced by this Japanese operation in Southeast Asia, takes a heavy toll on forests around the world. (Photo by Timothy J. Synnott.)

exporters. Selective purchasing is perceived as a market opportunity, a kind of positive discrimination in favor of management, while bans are perceived as political intervention, especially when they are aimed only at tropical forests and not at the equally abused temperate forests. Neither the threat nor the opportunity has yet done much to increase the areas of effective management, but this new market pressure is the most powerful force now operating in favor of forest management—certainly more powerful than offers of aid and technical assistance.

Unfortunately, the exercise of this buying power may have unanticipated results. For example, you may decide not to buy old-growth Douglas fir (*Pseudotsuga menziesii*) in order to protect the spotted owl and its habitat. But the alternative may be lauan plywood (*Shorea* spp.), made from dipterocarp timbers logged in the habitat of the Philippine monkey-eating eagle. If you decide that your new front door should not be made of mahogany (*Swietenia* spp.), the alternative may be milled from the ancient oaks in the mountains nearby.

The relationship between tropical- and temperate-wood consumption has been evident for years. As industrialized countries could afford to dedicate more of their forests to conservation and recreation, they began to satisfy demands by importing tropical timbers, effectively exporting their deforestation. Now, with dealers beginning to steer clear of controversial tropical timbers, the price and demand for temperate oak (*Quercus* spp.), cherry (*Prunus* spp.), and beech (*Fagus* spp.) are growing.

Individual companies can exert their influence directly on the management of tropical and temperate forests through wood-buying policies. The first step is for the company to write a clear buying policy and distribute it widely among its clients and suppliers. The hard part is to design a buying policy that helps conserve forests, rather than increases forest destruction. I propose the following main elements in a company buying policy:

1. All the forests supplying timber to the company must be identified by name and location, with information about the management and production system.

2. Only wood from well-managed forests will be bought. Well-managed forests are areas designated to remain as forest in perpetuity, where all activities fully comply with all national regulations, international agreements, and professional standards concerning harvesting, management, environmental protection, biological conservation, and the rights of workers and residents.

These guidelines have important implications. The company must know the names of all the forests providing its timber (feasible, though not always easy), but it is not required to label each piece of timber with the name of the individual forest that supplied it. In this way, a company can guarantee that all its timber comes from well-managed forests, without having to identify which forest supplied which board.

More important, this policy recognizes the web of national laws and agreements covering the basic elements of forest planning, management, and conservation. These laws are far from perfect, but they are comprehensive and part of the existing legal framework. United Nations agreements protect the rights of workers and indigenous people, and international agreements such as the Convention on International Trade in Endangered Species (CITES) identify and protect threatened species, including some timber trees. More than forty countries, including the United States, are members of the International Tropical Timber Organization (ITTO) and have agreed to limit their imports and exports of tropical timbers to the products of managed forests by the year 2000. These legal agreements are gradually leading to actions, and can be specified as conditions in wood-buying contracts.

There remains the delicate issue of how a buyer can be sure that the forest is managed according to the rules and norms. If a buyer is seriously concerned about the issues, it won't take long to form an opinion, based on information supplied by sources within the country of origin. If the buyer prefers to rely on a third party to evaluate the timber source, there is a growing number of certification organizations ready to evaluate or certify the state of forest management. These organizations review the environmental, ecological, social, and economic elements in light of the relevant laws, agreements, and technical and professional practices. If a buyer has to convince clients and the public, then the evaluating team or certifying company should be independent of all the main players, including the timber industry and government functionaries. (The Forest Stewardship Council is being set up to maintain the integrity and standards of accredited certifying companies.)

This sort of buying policy does not dictate how forests must be managed, but it makes it clear that the company will buy wood only from owners and governments that follow the rules and regulations. Many activists will argue that this is not enough. Doubtless, it won't be enough to protect every legitimate interest and every rare species. Nothing is ever quite enough. The combination, however, of buying policies that favor managed forests plus the promotion of lesser-used timbers would be a major contribution to both management and conservation, and it is perfectly feasible.

Consumers and conservationists are only just discovering what forest managers have long known. Simple wood-use decisions can have complicated social, economic, environmental, and political repercussions. Wrong decisions may do more harm than good, but that is no excuse for inaction. Especially, it is no excuse for waiting until the experts have all the information they need. None of us is likely to live that long. Certainly we must consider the situation carefully before taking action, but decisions have to be based on the best information and advice available at the time.

In the end, the future of forests, as of all natural resources, will depend on their being well managed. Good management may consist of total protection, where ecological and environmental factors are overwhelmingly sensitive and important. Many of the world's forests, however, are facing only two alternatives: total conservation or total clearance. In many of them, a combination of protection and production in perpetuity will be the best option.

Forest management for timber production has played and will continue to play a vital role in forest conservation throughout the world. Timber buyers can have an enormous influence in making sure that better management takes place, whatever wood they use and wherever it comes from. Don't underestimate that influence. ▲

From Circumstantial to Managed Conservation

The mahogany forests of Quintana Roo, Mexico

Laura K. Snook

Over the centuries the massive mahogany trees of Quintana Roo, Mexico, have been transformed into Mayan trading canoes, Spanish altars, English and American furniture, and Mexican plywood. Today, the extraction of mahogany provides the economic foundation for fifty rural communities involved in the Plan Piloto Forestal, widely regarded as a promising model for sustainable tropical forestry.

Mahogany grows intermixed with more than a hundred other tree species in the seasonal tropical forests of central and southern Quintana Roo, the Mexican state that comprises the eastern portion of the Yucatan peninsula. The most abundant tree in these forests is the chicozapote or sapodilla (*Manilkara zapota*), the source of chicle latex, which is used to make chewing gum.

Periodically, the forests are hit by hurricanes that damage or destroy trees on thousands of acres. During the dry season, which in some years approaches a drought, local farmers clear their agricultural fields by fire, which sometimes spreads into the neighboring forest. In posthurricane years, when the leaves, branches, and fallen trees provide abundant fuel, these fires can burn huge areas.

Bigleaf mahogany (*Swietenia macrophylla*) is the monarch of the Mexican rainforest. Its leaves turn red and drop during the dry season, when its woody, pear-shaped fruits open and shed their winged seeds. (Photo by Scott Landis.)

These conflagrations provide ideal conditions for the establishment of mahogany forests. Mahogany trees have strong wood, very few branches, and thick bark that permit them to survive both hurricanes and fires better than most other species. The survivors shed winged seeds that are dispersed by the wind over hundreds of yards. Mahogany seedlings thrive in full sun in clearings where they don't have to compete with preexisting seedlings or saplings of other species. As a result, the new forest stands that regenerate naturally after severe forest fires include a high density of mahoganies—about 25 per acre—growing among about 225 trees of other species.

Most of the mahoganies harvested today regenerated centuries ago in response to the chance events of hurricane and fire. Technological and socioeconomic factors also contributed, in unintended ways, to the conservation of the forests of Quintana Roo. During the first few centuries of logging, men felled the trees with axes and hauled the huge trunks to the nearest bodies of water, where they could be floated to their destinations. So, only trees within a few hundred yards of a river or lagoon were extracted. When oxen were introduced in the nineteenth century, this distance increased to three miles, and in the twentieth century, crawler tractors made it possible to fell trees up to thirty-five miles from water. It wasn't until the 1940s that the construction of logging roads made it possible to remove mahoganies from almost any part of the forest.

Even then, mahoganies were protected from depletion by the high standards imposed on logs for export. Unless trees were large, straight, and completely solid, they were not accepted by the buyers for English and American timber companies. As a result, many mahogany trees were left standing in the forest because they were partially rotted or otherwise imperfect. These trees produced the seeds that grew into new mahoganies when hurricanes or fires provided favorable conditions for regeneration.

The abundance of chicozapote trees also contributed to forest conservation in Quintana Roo. At the end of the nineteenth century, chicle-latex tappers migrated from other parts of the country during the six-month rainy season. They established camps in the national forests and collected the chicle latex to sell to the

have enough land for both agriculture and forestry. Second, because these communities have permanent rights to their forest land and stand to benefit in the long term from their resources, they have conserved the forest to maintain their chicle trees.

The mahogany forests of Quintana Roo have also been conserved as the result of specific conservation policies. According to the Mexican Constitution, forests belong to the whole nation. Therefore, regardless of land ownership, all forests in Mexico are managed according to guidelines defined by national forestry laws. These laws require that forest studies and management plans define how many and what sizes of trees can be harvested each year. Licensed foresters must mark the trees to be harvested, and permits must be obtained before timber can be transported. A surcharge is levied on each cubic meter of timber harvested to cover the costs of forest studies, timber-marking, and replanting.

These controls were first imposed on timber-harvesting in Quintana Roo in the 1950s, when the Mexican government established a veneer plant in the area so they could process mahogany timber domestically. For twenty-five years, this government plant held a concession to harvest the mahogany trees on one million acres of forest land within their radius of supply. Although these lands had already been granted to communities, the communities were not permitted to process their mahogany timber or to sell it to anyone other than the government. Communities were paid a low price set by the government, and many people earned daily wages working in the logging industry. Under this system, however, the communities were not earning enough to consider timber a potential foundation for their economies.

chewing-gum industry in the United States. In the 1930s, in part to populate their border with the colony of British Honduras, Mexico's Agrarian Reform program granted large tracts of land to communities of chicle tappers, calculating that each tapper required 850 acres of forest to make a living. As a result of this policy, forest communities in this region today each control an average of 50,000 acres of land, of which 20,000 acres are forested. This amounts to 280 acres of land, including 110 acres of forest, per family.

This form of land and forest ownership has contributed to forest conservation in two ways. First, population density is low, so people

In 1983, the government's mahogany concession ended, as did many similar government timber concessions nationwide. During the concession period, conflicts between government industries and forest communities had erupted all over Mexico, and many communities had refused to sell their timber at all rather than accept low government prices. Recognizing that the concession system had neither succeeded in ensuring sources of supply for state-owned industries, nor provided sufficient rural development benefits for local people, the government granted the forest

communities the right to harvest, transform, and sell the timber from their own forest lands.

The Plan Piloto Forestal has helped organize the forestry communities of Quintana Roo to take advantage of this period of change. Communities have banded together in five associations that pay foresters to carry out the legally required forest studies, obtain permits, and supervise timber-harvesting and reforestation. They have obtained credit to buy chainsaws, winches, skidders, and trucks to extract timber, and a few of the larger communities have

installed sawmills so they can process their logs and sell boards. Recently, carpentry workshops have been integrated into sawmills, to produce mahogany doors from sawn boards and beehives and simple chairs from mahogany scraps that were formerly burned.

(left) Value-added processing injects more money into the local economy and provides an important incentive for forest management. At Caobas, one of the participating communities in the Plan Piloto Forestal, workers fit a bandsaw blade in preparation for milling lesser-known hardwood species. (Photo by Scott Landis.)

(above) Sawn mahogany lumber, sold in large quantity on the local market, is stacked for drying. (Photo by Scott Landis.)

These developments have provided forestry employment for most members of communities with the largest and richest forests, while increasing many times over their earnings from timber-harvesting.

In addition to the lumber industries, the forestry activities of the Plan Piloto communities—such as the tapping and sale of chicle latex, the felling of trees of various hardwood species and the production of railroad ties, the hunting of wildlife for meat, and the production and sale of honey from forest beehives—are important sources of income and subsistence goods. Because their economies depend on all of these activities, the communities recognize the importance of safeguarding the future productive capacity of their forests.

The management of these complex tropical forests for sustained yields of mahogany timber represents a considerable challenge, however. To be sustainable, timber-harvesting must be in balance with the rate of replacement of trees through growth and regeneration. Recent research indicates that mahogany trees require more than 120 years to achieve the current commercial diameter of 22 inches. This means that harvests that take more than $1/120$ of the mahogany volume from a forest each year are exceeding replacement rates. Current harvesting plans, based on overly optimistic estimates of a seventy-five-year rotation, are removing mahoganies twice as fast as their growth rate. To ensure sustainable future harvests of mahogany, forest owners must greatly reduce their annual cuts. Mahogany is of course only one of many tree species in the forest. The drastic reduction in its harvest, which could result in a painful adjustment in local income, is one of several management options available. To maintain a reasonable income at a lower rate of harvesting, they must have extensive forests and invest in sufficient timber-processing to increase the value of each log harvested.

Waiting for mahogany trees to grow to commercial size is only part of the sustainability problem. It is even more difficult to recreate, through forestry practices, the clearings necessary for mahogany trees to regenerate. One of the principal obstacles is the abundance of associated tree species that are not recognized as commercial timbers. According to current logging practices, all mahoganies

larger than the minimum commercial diameter are felled in each year's cutting area, an average of only one tree in every two acres. This selective system leaves standing hundreds of trees of other species on each acre. The crowns of these trees produce shade and their roots occupy the soil, so mahogany seedlings are unable to become established and grow, even when planted in logged areas. Unless markets can be developed for these currently noncommercial species so they can be profitably logged, creating open areas for mahogany regeneration is too costly a process. It is crucial for forest management and for the future of the mahogany forest that lesser-known tropical woods be accepted by consumers.

If markets for other species were sufficiently developed, forest-management options would greatly increase. Groups of trees could be logged in patches, recreating the conditions produced by hurricanes. Mechanical methods could then be employed to imitate the effects of fire, controlling competition from sprouts, seedlings, and saplings. Parent trees of mahoganies and other species, retained around the logged patch, would reseed a new mixed-species forest in the open areas. Aided by these harvesting and silvicultural techniques, each year new patches would be harvested and new forests would reseed. Such a system should increase mahogany densities fiftyfold, without losing the current species mixture. Furthermore, because species other than mahogany account for most of the wood volume in the forest, the sale of other timber species would greatly increase the potential annual income from timber-harvesting. This would truly be forest conservation by design.

In centuries past, the mahogany forests of Quintana Roo maintained themselves as a result of technological and market limitations, and chance climatic events. Now these forests must be sustained through the deliberate efforts of the Plan Piloto Forestal communities to balance timber-harvesting with growth rates and to ensure regeneration. The ability of these communities to manage their forests sustainably, however, is closely linked to the tropical timber trade. Timber buyers must recognize that silvicultural management, which is necessary to ensure the future of the forest, requires a substantial investment. In the interest of sustaining timber supplies over the long term, consumers should be willing to

pay more for timber from managed forests, which otherwise cannot compete with wood mined from virgin forests with no regard for the future, and to purchase products made from lesser-known tree species.

It is clear that the diversity and ecology of these forests represent significant conservation challenges, but the alternative to investing in forest management is to risk mining out mahoganies. Once these valuable trees are depleted, the forest will have so little commercial value that alternative land uses, such as cattle pasture, will appear, in

An employee of the Plan Piloto Forestal points to lesser-known hardwoods milled and stacked for export. Mahogany is only one of hundreds of hardwood tree species in the forests of Quintana Roo. Forest-management options will increase dramatically if markets for other tree species can be developed. (Photo by Scott Landis.)

the short term, to be more profitable. And if these tropical forests are transformed, not only mahoganies, but hundreds of other species—from toucans to monkeys—that currently depend on them for habitat will be lost. ▲

A Landscape without Lines
The Collins Almanor Forest

Roy Keene

On the pumice terraces under Mount Lassen, the southernmost volcano of the Pacific Cascade Range, a continuous forest spreads like a great blanket. Many early timbermen, latecomers to the rugged interior of northern California, logged this forest selectively and with a lighter hand than those in other regions. In the last century, some parts of this forest became federal reserves and so were spared the axe; others were carefully thinned to produce a steady supply of timber.

Flying overhead, it is difficult to see where Mt. Lassen National Park meets the private Collins Almanor Forest (CAF). Fifty years of active logging in the CAF has had a minimal impact on the landscape, whereas in the Cascade forests to the north, highly visible "cookie-cutting" threatens the biological integrity of the forestscape and catalyzes conflicts over forest use.

Forests are a fusion of soil, seed, and climate. The soils of the 91,000-acre CAF are constituted from weathered volcanic rocks in the north, and batholithic granitic rocks in the south. The average elevation of the CAF is 4,800 feet, and most of the 50 inches of average annual precipitation occurs as snow—there was 8 feet of it

on the ground at one time last year. Because the porous soils do not retain water and the summers are often long and dry, moisture stress and fire danger are common seasonal forest conditions. As a result, over time, the CAF has evolved into a pine-dominated, mixed conifer forest, with trees such as true fir (*Abies concolor*) and incense cedar (*Libocedrus decurrens*) competing for space in the understory.

Prior to 1900, both natural and human-caused fires swept the CAF regularly, creating open, parklike stands of fire-resistant large pine (mainly *Pinus ponderosa*) and true fir. The effect of ninety years of active fire suppression in the Sierras has since caused a serious ecological shift in undisturbed areas, most easily recognized by replacement of pine with fir.

Wildlife and associative vegetation are controlled by the dynamics of fire disturbance just as much as by tree composition. Deer, coyotes, mountain lions, grosbeaks, jays, and robins prefer the wide-spaced trees and meadows associated with regular fire regimes. Nitrogen-cycling shrubs such as ceanothus, forage plants such as gooseberry and elderberry, grasses, and wildflowers all require open sites and sun. Without the action of fire—nature's "reset" button—open and diverse forest stands turn into dark, crowded thickets.

In most of the West, the development of the timber industry was dependent on the establishment of the railroads. In the early twentieth century, the great northern California pine plateau was finally connected by rail to more populated areas in the central valley. As mills like Red River Lumber Company moved into the area, timber stands were high-graded for pine at a rapidly increasing rate. Everett Collins, originally from Pennsylvania, had acquired most of the CAF lands by the turn of the century, but waited patiently for the right time to begin harvesting. By World War II, when most of the adjoining private pine forests had been cut out and lumber prices were rising exponentially, the Collins family decided to begin harvesting timber strategically from the CAF. Before making this first cut, however, they had already enjoyed the benefits of twenty years of research and study in Sierran pine forests, and the wisdom of CAF's first forester, Waller Reed.

Open, parklike stands of large pine and fir characterize much of the Collins Almanor Forest. Thanks to selective thinning of crowded or weaker trees, the quality of the forest and the diversity of species have not changed much since this photo was taken in 1924. (Photo courtesy of Trygve Steen and The Collins Pine Company.)

Whether or not formally stated, forest management inevitably addresses two critical land-use questions: for what and for whom will the resource be managed. Management is molded by the beliefs and the bias of the forester in charge, and Waller Reed's vision of sustainable forestry clearly enunciated "for what and for whom" he intended to manage the Collins family holdings. In an application for tree-farm status, submitted in the 1940s, Reed wrote:

Management for the area embraced in the Collins Almanor Forest is so planned that in the minimum of time as is possible the area will be placed upon a sound, economic sustained yield basis. Through the application of sound forestry practice, entailing the use of proper selective logging, fire and insect protection, maximum utilization and care for the reserve stands of timber, a continuous

supply of logs and other forest products will be assured. This continuous flow of forest wealth will make for a high standard and stabilized community which in turn will not only benefit the community itself, but the County, State and Nation as a whole.

(CAF Forestry Staff, *Collins Almanor Forest: 51 Years of Forest Management* [Chester, Calif.: Collins Almanor Forest, 1991], p. 32)

Foresters like Waller Reed knew that maintaining the long-term health of the Sierra forest required forestry operations that physically (if not chemically) mimicked fire. By the 1940s, research foresters had developed a tree-selection system that considered a tree's vigor, dominance, age, crown condition, and needle density. By observing these indicators of tree health, CAF foresters could select crowded or weaker trees for cutting before they became "detonators" for voracious beetle populations. Then, as now, trees at a high risk of mortality were cut throughout the forest and stands were selectively thinned to reduce the unnatural competition caused by fire suppression.

Sustained yield—the continual balance of growth against harvest—is achieved through accurate measurement and simple calculations. The progress of forestry manipulations on the CAF is charted by regular measurements of tree growth on 552 well-distributed, one-acre plots throughout the forest. Data collection is enhanced by photographs taken over a span of more than forty years. The plots are treated and harvested in the same manner as the general forest. The amount of timber to be harvested each decade is projected from the average net growth recorded throughout the inventory plots.

Fifty years of careful thinning have produced a forest that is today obviously managed, but reasonably pleasing to the eye, and relatively unaffected by the health problems that plague undisturbed parts of the adjacent Mt. Lassen National Forest. It is still moderately stocked with mature saw-timber, and it is growing in volume four times as fast as when management began. After removing 1.5 billion board feet over a fifty-year period, at the rate of roughly 30 million board feet per year, the standing timber volume remains 1.5 billion board feet! This is a classic example of sustained-yield forestry.

Although CAF foresters still use the same basic selection system in marking trees for harvest, they have rapidly embraced the latest developments in forest science. Their actions show that they value soil productivity, watershed vitality, and wildlife diversity as much as they value timber. For example, foresters have changed procedures in order to retain more standing dead timber (snags) and fallen woody debris, which provide the necessary habitat for a variety of animal species, such as woodpeckers. Under the frugal mortality-risk harvest system, snags were rarely left in the forest. Now, snags

and live trees for future snags are deliberately planned for and retained, as are increased levels of ground-level waste wood.

Perhaps the greatest economic evidence of the success of sustainable forestry in the CAF is the health of the adjoining community of Chester, California. Chester has enjoyed the benefits of a relatively steady forest-industry payroll for fifty years. In spite of recent layoffs resulting from modernization of the mill, the citizens of Chester have the highest regard for the company and the forest. The community also reaps noneconomic benefits—the CAF is left open and ungated for everyone to enjoy.

The Collins sawmill has historically produced half of its quality finished pine lumber from logs from the CAF and half from logs from nearby public forest lands. About ten years ago, the mill began to use "whitewood," primarily white, or true, fir, which allowed harvesters to gradually shift their reliance from large trees to the smaller trees that crowd the understory. This opportunity to utilize fire-suppressed ingrowth was further enhanced by the addition of a state-of-the-art cogeneration plant to produce electrical power from wood waste. Previously unmarketable thickets of small trees could now be profitably thinned and chipped. In the process of becoming more automated, the mill has become more efficient.

Both pine and whitewood are sawn, kiln-dried, resawn, planed, trimmed, and often further milled to create value-added products like finger-jointed molding stock. Years of quality-oriented production have created dependable building products that are consumed by wholesalers as quickly as they roll off the belt. Over the past few years, the company has continually added equipment and skilled operators to their manufacturing line. Eventually, Collins managers plan to build up the work force by increasing their value-added operations.

Scientific Certification Systems (SCS) has recently certified the CAF forest (and products milled from CAF timber) as a sustainable forestry operation. As an experienced private forester in the Pacific West and an inspection team member, I can say that the CAF came through a rigorous analysis with flying colors. There are not likely to be very many commercial forests west of the Rocky Mountains that

The Collins Pine mill is surrounded by an otherwise unbroken sea of green, running to the base of Mt. Lassen in Northern California. (Photo courtesy of Tryg-Sky/Lightl lawk.)

Today, Collins's owners and managers, and the forest itself, face a new challenge. In producing over 65 million board feet of lumber per year, the Collins mill relies on the surrounding national forests to provide half of the logs required to maintain its two daily shifts. The available supply of mature pine is rapidly dwindling in surrounding public forests. A temporary restriction imposed by the U.S. Forest Service now limits national forest green-tree sales to trees with a diameter of less than 30 inches at breast height. The restriction was in response to recommendations by a team of scientists enlisted to prescribe methods of maintaining minimum forest habitat for the southern spotted owl. (This owl has been thriving in CAF's well-kept stands for years.)

Faced with a decrease in public timber supplies as well as the possibility of additional regulatory restriction on cutting big pines on their own lands, a company executive was asked by a member of SCS's inspection team whether or not Collins would depart from sustained yield on CAF to make up for public-forest shortages. He responded that they would continue just as they always had—prudently taking the interest produced by a well-kept forest, without liquidating the capital itself, even if it meant reducing the mill to one shift. This willingness to manage for a healthy forest instead of for maximum profit is, I believe, the keystone of sustainable industrial forestry. ▲

will rate higher than this well-kept and tested example of prudent forestry. It is one thing to manage a small "hobby" woodlot with a set of tight constraints for a few years; it is quite another to successfully maintain a 92,000-acre forest for fifty years while pumping a steady flow of timber to the mill. In sustainable-forestry operations, the passing of time and the ability to satisfy a prudent demand for timber without compromising the ecological integrity of the forest are the tests of silvicultural success.

(left) More than fifty years of active logging and careful pruning have produced a healthy, but obviously managed forest, moderately well stocked with mature saw-timber. (Photo by Trygve Steen.)

(above) A large saw for old-growth timber at the Collins Pine Company Mill in Chester, California. (Photo courtesy of Trygve Steen.)

(right) Certified as "State-of-the-Art Well-Managed" in 1993 by Scientific Certification Systems (SCS) of Oakland, California, Collins Pine will be marketing its lumber in retail outlets across the country. The "State-of-the-Art" designation on this label indicates that the Collins Pine Company Mill falls within the top ten percent of forestry operations participating in the SCS certification program. (Label courtesy of Scientific Certification Systems.)

CERTIFIED

This wood was harvested from a State-of-the-Art Well-Managed Forest*

SCIENTIFIC CERTIFICATION SYSTEMS

* Collins Pine Co., Chester CA Div.
Collins Almanor Forest

Certification Scores:	
SUSTAINABLE HARVEST	86
ECOSYSTEM HEALTH	81
COMMUNITY BENEFITS	89
(100 = Maximum Possible Score)	

A Century of Forest Stewardship
The Menominee Forest of Wisconsin

Scott Landis

*A*web of blacktop stretches across central Wisconsin. From the Mississippi River in the west to Green Bay and Lake Michigan in the east, the roads are laid out in a surveyor's grid and named with letters of the alphabet. When the planners ran out of letters, they simply doubled them up. The towns and counties these roads stitch together bear the Indian and French names of an earlier era: Oshkosh and Winnebago, Eau Claire and Marinette.

The tree-lined borders of the Menominee Indian Reservation, a 234,000-acre rectangle of forested land, not far from Green Bay, appear as linear as any county road. In the wintertime, they are so crisply defined against the surrounding snowy fields that I'm told they have been used to focus the lenses of orbiting satellite cameras. The reservation is home to about 4,000 Menominee and is the largest contiguous block of sustainably managed timber in the northern Lake States.

Diversity of species is increasingly recognized as a yardstick of forest vitality. Through seed dispersal, pollination, and the laws of the food chain, the largest tree or mammal may depend upon the smallest insect or plant for its survival. Single-species plantations have played an important role in wood-fiber production, but they are capable of supporting only a limited range of plant and animal life and they are highly susceptible to disease. The Menominee reservation contains eleven of the fifteen major forest-habitat types in Wisconsin and more than twenty-five commercial species of timber, including hard and soft maple (*Acer* spp.), red oak (*Quercus* spp.), white pine (*Pinus strobus*), and hemlock (*Tsugas canadensis*). All original timber species still flourish, except for elm (*Ulmus* spp.).

As lush as the Menominee forests are, they are hardly pristine. Every road leads to skidder tracks and stumps. The reservation is managed intensively for both hardwood and softwood saw-timber and pulp. The Menominee harvest between 20 and 30 million board feet of lumber every year—altogether more than 2 billion feet since cutting began in 1865. The most recent forest inventory indicates a higher volume and quality of saw-timber now than when the land was first surveyed.

The Nicolet National Forest, which abuts the northeast border of the reservation, includes similar terrain, soils, and timber species,

---

For more than a century, the Menominee Indian forest and mill have been the lifeblood of the community. The Menominee harvest between 20 and 30 million board feet of lumber each year, consisting of more than twenty-five different native hardwood and softwood species. (Photo by Scott Landis.)

(above) The Menominee manage about 1,000 acres of white-pine forest under a shelterwood program that mimics the natural fire-succession sequence. (Photo by Scott Landis.)

(right) Menominee crews are well trained and carefully monitored in order to minimize damage to the soil and to surrounding unmarked timber. (Photo by Scott Landis.)

but it was cut over and burnt to sod in the last century. Although its commercial forest is more than twice the size of the Menominee Reservation, Nicolet is not nearly as rich or diverse. In a 1984 report that compared the productivity of the Menominee and Nicolet forests, the area forestry supervisor for the Wisconsin Department of Natural Resources, Kenneth Sloan, reported that the Nicolet forest produces only slightly more sawn timber and pulpwood than the Menominee and about half the volume of high-quality saw logs. In a recent conversation I had with Sloan, he noted that the Menominee Reservation is "really a gold mine, a laboratory" for sophisticated forest-management techniques. "They're about fifty years ahead of everyone else," he said. "When we're planting, they're thinning. When we're thinning, they're worried about regeneration...." The Menominee forest may be the antithesis of wilderness—land left alone to take care of itself—but it is one of the best examples of sustainable development I've found.

In his environmental classic, *A Sand County Almanac,* Aldo Leopold wrote that the best definition of a conservationist "is written not with a pen, but with an axe. It is a matter of what a man thinks about while chopping, or while deciding what to chop." A professional forester at the University of Wisconsin and one of the fathers of modern conservation, Leopold was concerned with restoring ecological integrity where it had been undermined and maintaining the fragile balance of diversity where human beings had intruded. In short, he was describing the kind of stewardship that is practiced on the Menominee reservation, four counties to the northeast of Leopold's sand-farm retreat. But in the Menominee forests, such decisions are not left to the man who wields the chainsaw. Modern forestry has become a lot more complicated.

Marshall Pecore is forest manager of Menominee Tribal Enterprises (MTE), the business arm of the tribe that oversees its woodlands and sawmill operations. Pecore is widely respected for his ability to mediate the often divergent interests of the community, tribal officers, MTE foresters and their counterparts in the Bureau of Indian Affairs and Wisconsin Department of Natural Resources. Together, these parties share responsibility for feeding the

Menominee sawmill, observing the allowable cut, and ensuring that the quality and diversity of the forests are preserved. MTE operations are ultimately responsible to a twelve-member Menominee board of directors, elected by the tribe. Between the sawmill and the woods, the enterprise employs about 200 people.

The bulk of the reservation, Pecore explains, is blanketed with northern hardwoods in an abundance of species. Along with white pine and hemlock, these so-called "tolerant" hardwoods are able to regenerate in their own shade, but do poorly in direct sunlight. They are managed in diverse stands of mixed species and ages. Roughly twenty percent of the reservation is managed for aspen (*Populus tremuloides*) and jackpine (*Pinus banksiana*) under an even-aged (clearcut) prescription. These shade-intolerant, pioneer species thrive in well-drained, sandy soils and full sunlight. Less than five percent of the total forest area is held in plantations.

Clearcuts are no less controversial on the Menominee reservation than elsewhere. They are ugly to look at and, when conducted on a grand scale (as in the Pacific Northwest or the Amazon basin), they have been rightly condemned for their attendant loss of diversity and animal habitat. According to Pecore, the issue is not that simple. In the natural succession of the Menominee forest, he explains, pioneer species like aspen and jackpine mature in fifty to eighty years. As they begin to deteriorate they give way to maple, the dominant climax species that grows up in their shade. Protected from fire, which has played a major role in Wisconsin forest succession for thousands of years, the reservation would be overrun by maple if left to its own devices.

To maintain softwood fiber production and to reap the long-term ecological benefits of a diverse mix of native timbers, the Menominee manage shade-intolerant species like aspen and jackpine in small clearcuts of not more than thirty acres in size. Such clearcuts are not contiguous and they're permitted only on high ground, well away from streams or lakes. This minimizes environmental damage and offers good cover for wildlife. Unlike clearcuts I've seen elsewhere on the continent, reservation clearcuts are not screened from public view by cosmetic buffer strips. As Pecore says, they've got nothing to hide.

Except for a brief period in the 1920s and 30s, when parts of the reservation were high-graded for old-growth white pine, the tribe has opted to leave the tall timber alone. But their two-step

shelterwood program, which artificially mimics the old fire-succession sequence, may point the way to successful pine regeneration. Once the pine seedlings have established themselves, they are protected from competition either by hand-brushing or by what MTE silviculturalist Steve Heckman calls the "prudent" application of herbicides. According to Heckman, in the absence of fire, "we do not have the methodology to regenerate white pine without chemicals." Even so, the Menominee turn to herbicides only as a "last resort." So far, the results are impressive. The reservation has roughly 1,000 acres of white pine under shelterwood management, and a second generation of pine is developing nicely beneath the high canopy. But, like clearcuts and prescribed burns, the herbicide program remains contentious among a number of community members who take a personal interest in the health of their forest. Pecore acknowledges the risk of using herbicides, but adds, "there's risk in everything you do."

Pecore's job—indeed the primary mission of his entire forest-management team—is to identify the areas best suited to each species and then to prescribe the most appropriate silvicultural treatment. Perhaps the most important tool at his disposal is the Continuous Forest Inventory, which is conducted every ten years on more than 800 permanent forest plots. The inventory provides a base of information against which MTE foresters can measure the long-term effects of growth, disease, and cutting on timber volume and quality, as well as on species diversity.

At the heart of the enterprise is a new computerized database, with which the management system is tailored to suit specific soil types and wildlife habitats. The reservation is divided into 109 compartments, or cutting units, but there may be as many as 15,000 different stands of trees, or "micro sites," in the forest. Where they once treated whole compartments under a single prescription, they can now begin to treat each stand.

Sophisticated software notwithstanding, Pecore admits that good forestry still boils down to "walking out in the field, identifying what you want to do and making judgment calls based on biological reality." Pecore's staff can do everything right on paper, but as Heckman says, "Once a tree is cut you can't stick it back. It's not

like a crop of corn," he says. "You screw it up this year, maybe you fix it in sixty, eighty, or a hundred years."

Steve Arnold—the only university-trained Menominee forester on the reservation, apart from Pecore—explains that two four-man Menominee marking crews spend all year in the bush, measuring and marking timber stands in advance of the cut. The trees they select can make or break the quality of the forest. They follow a conservative recipe that's the exact opposite of the so-called "selective" cut or high-grading practices that guide many conventional operations. "Instead of cutting the best," Arnold says, "we cut the worst."

"Collateral" damage is as much a part of logging as it is of war. An experienced logger intuitively computes wind speed and direction, the angle of lean, and the shape of the crown before he first plunges his saw blade into bark. But the process may be closer to art than science. With about fifty two-man logging crews operating at any time, things are bound to get messy. Falling timber lands on other trees. Skidders compact the soil, crush seedlings, and rip the bark off healthy, unmarked trees.

"Our goal is one thing and what our guys are doing in the woods is another," Pecore says. In a perfect world, crews would log only in the wintertime on frozen ground and with good snow cover. But loggers and millworkers have to eat all year. They operate in the summer, fall, and winter, with a lengthy shutdown during spring breakup, when the frost and snow leave the bush. The Menominee no longer use horses to haul their logs, but they are restricted to small skidders with rubber tires. To minimize damage, loggers are required to use permanent skid trails—a rarity in most production forests—and tree-length skidding is prohibited.

Loggers can be fined for excessive damage—as much as $250 for cutting a green, unmarked tree. Pecore reports that logging contractors are fined regularly for a variety of infractions, from lost logs to hauling too fast. Arnold and other foresters visit cutting sites at least twice a week to check on operations and they spend more time, if necessary, breaking in new loggers. All contractors are required to attend a training session during the spring shutdown.

Despite the regulations—which are among the tightest in the business—non-Menominee loggers compete for the chance to work on the reservation. In a recent report on Menominee forestry prepared for Scientific Certification Systems (SCS) of Oakland, California, a logger from neighboring Shawano is quoted as saying that "the Indians are more restrictive [than whites]...but I suppose I'd do it the same way if I owned that forest."

According to Bob Simeone, a Wisconsin forester and chief author of the SCS report, "When it comes to forest management, nobody holds a candle to these people, but their industry is Cro-Magnon." Their strategic access to the Wisconsin pulp market has provided a secure outlet for low-grade pulpwood—the Menominee sell to sixteen different mills within a 150-mile radius. But it offers little incentive for more valuable product development. Like a lot of American resource industries, the Menominee mill reflects a heavy investment in primary processing (saws, planers, and kilns) but almost nothing in secondary, value-added processing (plywood, veneer, furniture, and so on). "If [the Menominee] have any fault," Simeone says, "it's that they're too intense in their management." On the land he manages in northern Wisconsin, Simeone strives for about seventy percent utilization of the upland forests. The Menominee, he figures, use ninety-eight percent. "They could probably turn twice the profit with half the land under management, if they used more secondary processing."

It costs more to harvest a forest sustainably than not, but timber prices are set by demand and competition and by nationwide economic trends that are almost entirely blind to good management. Despite recent mill renovations and reductions in manpower, the enterprise lost money in all but four of the last thirteen years. The Menominee are not only saddled with the cost of intensive forest management, they have to sell whatever species and volumes their forest can sustainably yield. This resource-based, command economy calls for greater creativity than they've been able to muster thus far. In the recent recession, the Menominee were bolstered by their reputation for high-quality saw-timber and veneer logs, and their 1992 certification of sustainability (by SCS) may help them tap the rising consumer interest in "green" wood products. To stanch mill losses, they are also investigating specialty

markets in plywood, veneer, sawdust fuel pellets, and metric-dimension lumber for the Japanese.

In the short term, Pecore points out, they could return the enterprise to a positive cash-flow position simply by boosting the cut. "Tribal members could be really happy if we liquidated red oak—probably `til I went in the grave," he says. "But the next generation would pay."

Whatever triumphs or abuses the forest undergoes in the future, the fact that it is owned and managed by the community seems to ensure its survival. The Menominee reservation is the only one in the state not checkered with private land holdings and the only one in the country that maintains a "trust responsibility" with Congress to sustainably manage its own forests. Other industries may come and go—a new reservation casino already employs more people than MTE—but the role of the forest in the life of the community seems secure. As Steve Heckman explains, "We're managing this forest for the tribe forever. It's not a corporation, this is them."

However exemplary Menominee forest management, it represents only a small slice of the North American timber resource, very little of which is managed with the same long-range goals. Once lumber is processed at the Menominee mill, it is swallowed up in the continental maw of wholesale and retail lumber-marketing, where it remains undistinguished and essentially undistinguishable from carelessly managed wood. This is frustrating for the many woodworkers and consumers who are seeking responsible sources of managed timber.

Nobody knows how long the market will wait for well-managed products or how long the Menominee (and others like them) can afford to invest their forests with expensive management practices without tangible reward. If the Menominee experience is to be more than a noble experiment, we must act quickly to verify "good wood" claims and provide market access to well-managed forest products. Perhaps this exhibition and catalogue will help to educate the public about the need to do both. ▲

An article on this topic by Scott Landis appeared in *Harrowsmith Country Life* magazine in November, 1992.

THE WORK

Exhibition Criteria

Conservation by Design is an invitational and juried event. Twenty-eight of the seventy-six artists were invited to submit work. The others were accepted by jury.

Both juried and invited artists were asked to submit functional objects that address the interrelated issues of temperate and tropical wood consumption and responsible forest management. Entries were selected for their creative and aesthetically pleasing exploration of these issues. The use of certified, recycled, salvaged, or reconstituted material and of lesser-known or underused wood species was encouraged.

Artists were required to document the sources of supply for their materials. Each entry was further evaluated in light of the artist's written statement about the work and its relationship to the stated criteria.

Dimensions for each entry indicate outside measurements and are listed in the following sequence: height, width, depth or diameter.

Each piece is in the collection of the artist unless otherwise noted.

All photographs of artists' work are by Dean Powell unless otherwise noted.

The Jury

Edward S. Cooke, Jr.
Associate Professor
Department of the History of Art
Yale University

Silas Kopf
Director
Woodworkers Alliance for Rainforest Protection

Thomas S. Michie
Curator of Decorative Arts
Museum of Art
Rhode Island School of Design

Rosanne Somerson
Acting Head
Graduate Furniture Design Program
Rhode Island School of Design

Seth Stem
Associate Professor
Industrial Design Department
Rhode Island School of Design

Advisors

Ivan Ussach
Director
Woodworkers Alliance for Rainforest Protection

Mary Hallett
Rural Development Specialist
United States Forest Service

Mitchell Ackerman
b. 1955
Providence, Rhode Island

Pulp Hutch, 1993
Paper pulp, wire mesh, pine, copper, candles
61³/₄ x 42 x 34"

While traveling through northern India several years ago, I was astonished by the resourcefulness of the people. Virtually everything in India is recycled—felt tip pens are refilled and tin cans are transformed into toys. Sticks, clay, cow dung, hay, and found materials, such as mirrors, film canisters, and bottle caps, are used to create ornate and detailed pieces of shrinelike furniture.

The homes in the small villages I visited often had a hutch for storing grain and valuable things.

Intrigued with the idea of new beginnings for old materials, I made this hutch from paper pulp and recycled wood from crates and pallets. The shell is constructed of manila hemp paper that has been layered over a wire-mesh armature.

Peter Adams

b. 1946
Hobart, Tasmania, Australia

Forest Bench, 1993
Huon pine, myrtle
19⁵/₈ x 75 x 14¹/₂"
Lent by Daphne Farago

I believe that the development of ecodesign has to be inspired by the recognition of the deep interconnectedness—and interdependence—of all living things. It is not good enough anymore to just use the resources of this world, even in a sustainable manner, without understanding the full consequences—positive or negative—of

their removal for our use. A truly sustainable aesthetic demands that we come of age and start looking at the deeper significance of the objects we make, the materials they are made from, and the role they might play in the healing of this planet.

The wood used in this piece was salvaged from dam projects or clear-felling. Should it have been left to rot at the bottom of a lake or burnt in a Forestry Commission regeneration fire? I don't think so. For me, it is just as important that those trees that have fallen have as honorable an ending as possible. I pick up the felled tree bones of my myrtle and huon pine brothers and sisters, and cart them off feeling grateful that I

have the chance of extending their wood life a little longer. Maybe, when placed within an urban environment, their new bench form might in some small way be responsible for someone's reawakening.

If I could sit on a large eucalypt stump, close my eyes and go into the life within the dark of that ghost tree, could I not also—back home—sit in a wooden chair, close my eyes, and imagine I were back in the forest?

—excerpted from "Beyond Form and Function," *Habitat Australia*, July 1992.

Fred Baier

b. 1949
Pewsey, Wiltshire, England

Dual Quad, 1987
Birch plywood, steel, leather, pictorial
transfers, French polish
54 x 48 x 17"

Dual Quad is a roll-top drop-leaf transformer
robot desk. It is a robot driven by the forces of
good traveling through the universe promoting
the earth, which it does through a pictorial
collage covering its surface. It is made of
Scandinavian birch plywood, a highly sustainable
wood product, and is French polished. (There is
also in existence the hero's alter ego, driven by
the forces of darkness, who used to stalk *Dual
Quad* intent on capturing it and keeping earth's
secret for itself, but that piece was imprisoned
through purchase in a U.2 mill.)

There is no point in my waffling on about the
pros and cons of what wood to use. The way I
hear it, all arguments say it is important to
preserve our rainforests and tropical
hardwoods, so for *Dual Quad*'s sake, let's
preserve them. We should strive to be of our
time, making objects of our time, from materials
appropriate to our time. There is an abundance
of timber types that are still okay to use.
There are new materials to try out and new
processes to master. Skill and virtuosity need
not be undermined. Object makers should have
a sensitivity to materials and material
manipulation. It is their endeavor that creates
preciousness rather than the rarity of the stuff
from which things are made.

Photo by Karen Norguay.

Bruce Beeken
b. 1953
Jeff Parsons
b. 1956
Shelburne, Vermont

Hickory Chair, 1993
Hickory, hickory splint
33 x 20 x 18"

This chair was made of hickory harvested near
our shop on Shelburne Farms. The tree grew
nearby on the western slope of a wooded
moraine in the Lake Champlain basin. It was
removed to give a promising maple more room.
Were it not for a nearby sawmill, the tree
would have become firewood.

The modest diameter of this particular tree was
fine for the rather small billets that are
appropriate for chairs. The lumber was rift-sawn
and air-dried for several years. Most of the
curved pieces are steam-bent.

The woodlands at Shelburne Farms are managed
with three objectives: to promote recreational
use by humans, to preserve a balanced habitat
for a variety of wild animal species, and to
maintain a healthy forest, while maximizing the
growth potential of the economically more
valuable trees.

Garry Knox Bennett

b. 1934
Oakland, California

Slowly, Sorrow Fled The Village Again, 1991
Metal, plastic
60" h. (variable), 24" w. (variable)

I have never really been a "woodie." I have always felt that using wood for wood's sake was not that important to my furniture. With all of the reusable and renewable resources available to us today, there is no good purpose served by relying on rare and endangered species to make a piece of furniture important or beautiful. These ends can be achieved through good design and interesting use of available, renewable, and reusable materials.

I now recycle all of my Copenhagen tins and I no longer use toucan bills for drawer pulls.

Henry Black
b. 1947
Concord, New South Wales, Australia

Chainsaw, 1993
Ebony, purpleheart, rosewood, blackwood,
white beech, red cedar, holly, red oak veneer,
maple veneer, bark, newsprint, currency
Chainsaw: 10 x 44 x 10"
Pedestal: 25½" h., 13" dia.

This piece has been on my mind for ten years. It started in 1984 with an idea I had in Tasmania. In 1986 I made a mock-up and roughed out the body. Work was temporarily derailed for several reasons, including a decision by the New South Wales Woodworkers Association, of which I've been a member since 1979, to accept a large donation from the New South Wales Forestry Commission to stage a major exhibition. For the past one hundred years, the Forestry Commission has been responsible for the wholesale destruction of our local forest. Obviously, a piece like this wouldn't have been acceptable for their exhibition.

I made this piece from vanishing resources of exotic woods and from junk mail, hoping that people will really think about the politics of our resource use and management. The money and the bullets go together.

Michael Brolly
b. 1950
Hamburg, Pennsylvania

Our Mother Hangs In The Balance, 1992
Walnut, mahogany, holly, brass, veneers
12" h., 18³/₄" dia.
Lent by Dr. Irving Lipton

Bats are the so-called creatures of darkness, symbols of evil, bloodsucking enemies of humankind. Like the problems confronting our forests, these mammals are greatly misunderstood. They are voracious eaters of insects and play a major role in the propagation of many flowering plants.

This bat's 3-in. brass tongue holds it in the flower. Remove the bat, and the tree, which supports the plant, falls down—a symbol of the interconnectedness of all things and all actions. If we human beings continue our out-of-balance relationship with our planet, Mother Nature will compensate by swinging the pendulum to the opposite extreme, possibly eliminating the small environmental niche we need to survive.

The walnut is from a local hedgerow (complete with buckshot), the veneers were retrieved from the trash where I went to school.
I purchased the holly and the mahogany for the bat locally. The mahogany was part of a huge pile of checked and wormy stock, dumped at the local lumberyard and sold for eighty-five cents a board foot. (How much did the people in the country of origin get for cutting down those huge trees?)

I believe I did the right thing by saving these large timbers from becoming transient molding, turning them into beautiful objects that I hope will be cherished for a long time.

By displaying the objects made from these timbers, I try to evoke feelings of respect for nature, considerations of conservation, and reflections on the innate beauty of all that surrounds—not to incite the lust for mahogany at any cost.

Jon Brooks
b. 1944
New Boston, New Hampshire

Verde Styx Ladderback, 1993
Maple, colored pencil, lacquer
78 x 21 x 28"

My work has evolved from a subtractive process of carving massive logs into organic chair forms to a constructive process of creating nonfunctional chairs and sculpture from slender saplings and twigs. While teaching at the University of Tasmania, I challenged my students to build an all-wood, lightweight, functional chair. Through that experience, the *Verde Styx Ladderback* began. A recent commission for a dining set has started me on a group of chairs of which this is the first. In the construction and design I have paid attention to the traditional Shaker ladderback chair. My overall design is influenced by the material I find.

I live in the forest of New England, and the maple saplings I work with grow near my studio, are easily found, and are very renewable. Soon after I cut the saplings I remove the bark, bend the chair legs over forms, and dry them. I chose maple for its strength, durability, and longevity. The rung joints are fox-wedged and glued. The incised carving, colored with pencil, is a personal hieroglyphic style intended to convey the spiritual nature of my work. Poetic imagery and an emphasis on process and conservation are the ideas I seek to communicate.

Arthur Espenet Carpenter
b. 1920
Bolinas, California

Facet Table II, 1993
Alder, water-based finish
33 x 54 x 16"

This table is made from alder, a "weed" tree that grows in California bog lands. Too soft, too knotty, and too prone to warp for most furniture uses, it makes an excellent base for paint or other covering if used in thick planks. It's not too different from aspen and might be considered a poor man's poplar.

The water-based finish is presumably environmentally sound. At least it indicates that on the can. And the can is recyclable.

In general, I try to use California hardwoods, none of which seem to be endangered and none of which are of much commercial importance outside of California.

Now if I could only live without electricity and gasoline and the things they make go....

Polly Cassel
b. 1955
Northampton, Massachusetts

Rose's Finial Fantasy, 1993
Poplar, casein paint
74 x 24 x 11"

This cabinet—and all of my recent work—is made from poplar. Poplar tends to be underutilized by most furnituremakers because of its uneven coloration and uninteresting grain pattern. It is also one of the softest hardwoods and is considered less capable of sustaining wear.

In my work, these "undesirable" features are either superfluous or work to my advantage. All of my pieces are completely covered with paint, which eliminates the significance of the wood's color and grain structure. I texture my work, especially in the areas that are most susceptible to wear, and I do quite a bit of shaping and carving, so I actually prefer softer wood. I don't attempt to achieve a slick, stylized look in my work, so surface wear doesn't detract from the piece.

After I cover the wood with a base coat of paint, I treat it as an empty canvas. But I am not inclined to simulate either tropical or domestic woods. Instead, I prefer to create an entirely new surface that can be exotic, elegant, playful, bold, or subtle.

My choice of poplar was not initially a conscious political choice, but I'm pleased that it does not contribute to the devastation of the rainforests.

Martha Chatelain
b. 1935
Gary A. Zeff
b. 1944
Rancho Santa Fe, California

Nahele Keiki—Child Of The Forest, 1993
Macadamia, handmade paper of macadamia and cotton
Vessel: 7" h., 7¹/₂" dia.
Overall: 14 x 9 x 9"

Part of a grove of macadamia nut trees needed to be removed for a road to a housing project. The developer hoped to find a good use for the trees and contacted several woodworkers. Gary cut down one tree for woodturning, mindful of both the beauty of the radial lines of this native species and the propensity of this wood to check.

He made a hollow turning in the shape of a macadamia nut, leaving some bark attached. The form was turned while the wood was still wet and was carefully dried to prevent checking. The nut-shaped vessel is a representation of the tree itself.

Martha sculpted the surrounding leaves from the chips and shavings left over from the turning process. "The greatest influence on my artwork is the beauty I see in nature." She made the paper pulp by reconstituting the wood chips and shavings with cotton fibers in a hydropulper, and pulled sheets in a vat using the traditional mould and deckle. Water was extracted from the sheets by vacuum pressure, and the leaf shapes were sculpted while the paper was still damp.

Il Sang Cho
b. 1946
Pusan, Korea

Story, 1989
Zelkova
$10^3/_8$ x 29 x $4^1/_2$" (without base)

I treat woods not only as living creatures but also as partners with souls that come from mountains or earth. Every piece of my work is a dialogue between the soul of a tree and myself, in which I try to express the nature of life. The forceful stretching of trunks, the twistings and the many gnarls of branches inspire me to encounter difficult challenges or an unfavorable environment, while the gentle bendings and waving grains teach me to care for the wounded and to live with others in peace.

Through such dialogues, working with wood, I hope to send a message from the woods: they are now in great danger due to the negligence and greed of human beings.

Stephen Daniell
b. 1957
Easthampton, Massachusetts

Halo Desk, 1993
Curly yellow birch, cherry, pear, madrone
burl, maple and pear marquetry, leather
30 x 42 x 24"

Five years ago, I began a moratorium on the use
of tropical hardwoods. I had hoped simply to
educate myself to use exotic woods selectively
and responsibly, but instead I discovered the
complexity and intractability of the issues.
When I read that our New England scarlet
tanagers, which overwinter in the tropics, were
vanishing, I came to believe that popular
concerns about rainforest destruction were
not exaggerated.

Anything will sell if you veneer it in quilted
mahogany, and there is no substitute for the
visual orgy of a plank of old-growth Brazilian
rosewood. To stay in business, I decided to
develop designs, techniques, and materials
that would compete with the romance and
natural beauty of exotic tropical woods. To that
end, I have used layered gesso finishes,
iridescent glazes, metallic auto paint, light-
emitting diodes, colored epoxy, dyed woods and
veneers, temperate-wood burls, and
phosphorescent paint.

This piece can be considered complex work
with simple materials. The maple veneer in the
marquetry top and case is manipulated to create
the illusion of a three-dimensional ring.
The inside of each ring seems concave, the
outside convex. Each section has a highlight and
a shadow that will respond appropriately to a
light source. If a lamp is placed on the desk, the
rings will appear to be illuminated from that
point. This was achieved by cutting veneers on a
curve, starting from the edge of a solid, straight-
grained blank of maple. The arc of the curve
cuts across the grain in one direction, along the
grain, and then back across the grain in the
opposite direction. These thin slices were then
flattened, cut and assembled, with one side up

for the concave effect and the other side up for
the convex. In effect, I made my own curly maple,
but controlled the curl.

The rest of the marquetry employs natural
and dyed pear, handled in the traditional
manner. The leg caps are madrone burl, the

legs are curly birch; cherry and maple are
secondary woods.

I look forward to a future of more responsible
tropical-forest management. Meanwhile, there is
more than a lifetime's worth of other materials
at hand.

John Dunnigan
b. 1950
West Kingston, Rhode Island

Burnt Crate Cabinet, 1993
Recycled mahogany
32^1/$_2$ x 17 x 9"

The mahogany is from a shipping crate rescued out of a dumpster. I cut up the pieces, nailed the cabinet together, and then burned it. Have I thus prevented waste by making use of what would otherwise be trash?

As I watched the flames lap the edges of the cabinet, the following ideas chanted in my mind:

As long as the forests are wasted, the rivers and lakes are poisoned, and the air polluted, we must ask the questions again. Why? Who benefits? How?

As long as we allow extortion to continue in the form of jobs or progress versus conservation, and as long as we allow megabusiness to set the terms of the debate, we accept inevitable disaster.

As long as we support a diet that is wasteful of natural resources and energy, while at the same time being unhealthy, we will not thrive.

As long as we base our economy on mass production and planned obsolescence, we will be forced to consume raw materials insatiably until there are no more.

As long as humans believe that trees and indeed the entire living planet are merely resources to be exploited for profit, conservation by design or otherwise will not be effective.

In order for any of us to truly succeed, we must all succeed. Any serious discussion of conservation needs to include design in a political context. Right now, to be responsible designers, we need to have a political conscience.

David Ebner
b. 1945
Bellport, New York

Headboard, 1993
Sassafras
60 x 78 x 5"

Man's first furniture was likely made from the sticks and bones he found in his immediate surroundings. Likewise, the twisted sticks and spalted wood I use are found, native materials. The majority are sassafras, a fast-growing, underutilized native species, seldom employed for furniture.

My twisted-stick furniture puts no demand on the forest or lumber industries. These native spalted woods have all the richness and excitement of tropical woods, but are discarded natural materials at the end of their life cycles, which, if not used, would simply rot entirely.

David Ellsworth
b. 1944
Quakertown, Pennsylvania

Mo's Delight, 1993
White oak, multiple-axis turned and carved
7 x 8½ x 7"

The goal of all creative people is to make a statement through their work, such that their intent—the marriage between concept and content—is communicated by a synthesis of the material and the making process. But what happens if the beauty of the material (or the virtuosity of one's technique) so dominates the object that the statement becomes overwhelmed, even lost?

This dilemma is shared by all craftsmen who work in wood—our work is most often judged by the beauty of the material. This has contributed to the plight of the rainforest, the source of many woods that have come into high demand.

Mo's Delight—named for Mo Siegel, founder of the herbal tea company Celestial Seasonings, Inc.—was designed in response to this situation.

Rather than let the material be the inspiration for the design, I selected material to fit the design criteria. I looked for a wood species that is commonly available but not commonly used for other than utilitarian purposes, such as flooring and firewood. I chose white oak, not specifically to protest the use of rainforest timber, but because it is the ideal wood for the project. The grain patterns encircle the form in a balanced rhythm (a more "exotic" grain might decorate the surface, but detract from the form). The skinlike texture of the oak gives the impression that the spout and handles protrude from within the form. With all vessels, I am concerned with a feeling of containment, in which the source of the object's energy—its power—emanates from some unknown internal point.

To the classic issue of "form versus function," I can only express my pleasure in constructing an object that has all the necessary elements of a normal, functioning teapot, but which is clearly nonutilitarian (although someone no doubt will try to prove me wrong).

Glenn Elvig
b. 1953
Minneapolis, Minnesota

When A Tree Falls In The Forest, 1989
Basswood, maple, ear protectors
76 x 16 x 16"

When a tree falls in the forest it does make a
noise. A deafening noise. We can choose to
hear it or not.

Think about the silence of a seed, which sends
out its first root, feeling its way, silently
searching for the nutrients that sustain life.
The tree grows, quietly spending its life doing
tree things, occasionally making the obligatory
creaking and groaning sounds of its trunk and
limbs when blown by an overly aggressive wind.
The loudest noise a tree makes comes at the
end of its life, the crashing end induced by man
or old age.

Cutting down a tree is not morally wrong.
What is wrong is not trying to leave our planet
in a better—or at least no worse—condition
than we found it. A planet with quietly, quietly
growing trees.

Replant.

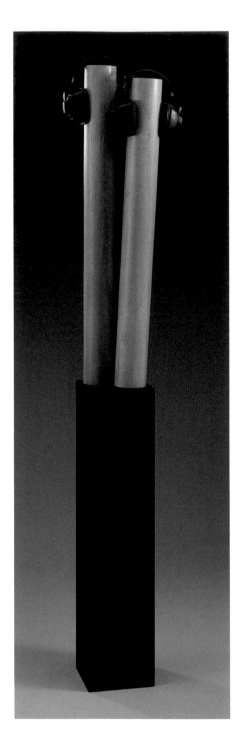

J. Paul Fennell
b. 1938
Topsfield, Massachusetts

Fleur De Neon II, 1991
Curly maple, neon, aluminum
11" h., 4" dia.

This lathe-turned, hollow vessel uses salvaged material from a woodcutter's lot, and demonstrates that turners need not rely on commercial sources of wood for their creative endeavors. Nor do we need to use exotic woods for spectacular color or figure.

In an urban environment, trees are often cut down to clear land or to remove storm-damaged or diseased specimens. This creates an opportunity for the turner to obtain wood at little or no cost, while remaining outside of the loop of commercial exploitation and consumption of forest resources. Indeed, the staggering number of trees cut down and left to clog our landfills—or, at best, to be burned as firewood—can easily fulfill the needs of the most prolific turner.

The objects I make focus attention directly on the beauty and sensuality inherent in the wood. By elevating the public's appreciation for and love of this material and by informing people of the sources of my material, I hope to create a reverence for all woods.

David Fobes
b. 1953
San Diego, California

Construction Work, 1992
Douglas fir, shop scrap wood, cement bags,
black tile grout, plywood, water-based IPN
finish
16 x 30 x 30"
Lent by Dr. Douglas Simay

Recycling, salvaging, and scavenging are central
to the creation of my furniture. I am intrigued
by the creation of decorative art from the waste
of an industrial and consumptive society. As an
artist living in the border region of San Diego/
Tijuana, I am constantly impressed by the

recycling ingenuity that occurs south of the
border. Coat hangers and cardboard oil cans are
transformed into colorful sun parasols. Old tire
tread becomes sandal soles. Paper bags that
contained cement to make concrete tiles are
recycled to package the finished product.
These are not "feel good" efforts or "green"
marketing strategies. They are symptoms of and
direct remedies for an economy in crisis.

Construction Work criticizes the condition of the
ecosystem not by representation, but by being a
direct and viable solution. The piece uses
recycled or salvaged materials and plywood.
The billboard paper was scavenged after periods
of rain and provides free and wonderful surfaces
for plywood substrates.

Once I became conscious of the rainforest
crisis, I began to realize that the problem is the
whole of our human activity and its impact on
the environment. In this spirit, I have abandoned
petroleum- and chemical-based adhesives, and I
substitute water- and protein-based paints and
coatings for all interior projects.

In my entire lifetime I will not be able to recycle
or salvage a single landfill of waste. Still, by
creating furniture and art from a coalition of
salvaged, low-impact materials, with ecocentric
intention, I aim to reduce the adverse impact of
my community on the environment.

Eck Follen
b. 1953
New Bedford, Massachusetts

Musical Chair, 1993
Steel rod
27 x 40 x 32"

There is an element of risk in making a metal chair for a show about wood. Surely it will be perceived as a flippant solution to a serious situation, which is far from the truth. Steel, whose production and use have their own environmental bugaboos, certainly can't be considered a viable substitute for wood, however it does open a new window on our perceptions of beauty and value.

To most people, furniture = wood, good furniture = good wood, and, of course, the best furniture = the best wood. For this chair, I combined a common construction material with the one completely limitless resource—human imagination—to make something provocative and desirable. In the end, the only difference between this chair and a pile of sticks is in our associations with the material.

It is commonly held that the less available a thing is, the more beguiling it becomes—this is as true for natural resources as it is for money, power, and sex. It seems a pervasive standoff of the human condition. The future of all our resources (human as well as natural) might lie in learning to value without needing to own, to see beauty and value not just in the objects or materials themselves, but in how they are made and used, and to honor vision, connection, and ingenuity just as much as ebony.

As my mother used to tell me (to a completely different end), it's not what you've got, it's how you use it.

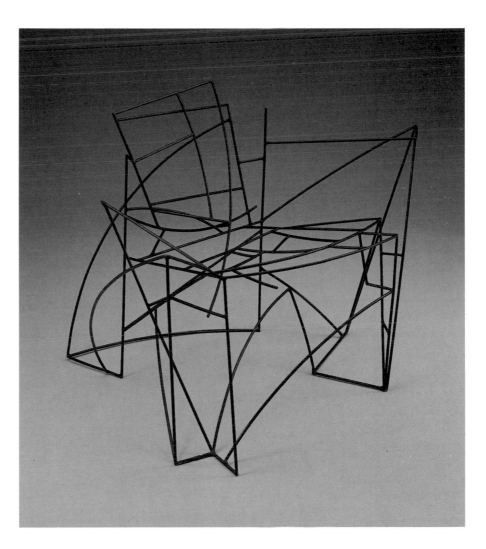

W. Logan Fry
b. 1944
Richfield, Ohio

Spectre Of A Distant War, 1991
Found wood, plywood, dowels, acrylic paint,
polyurethane
24 x 14 x 6"
Illustrated

Maple Tree's Silent Scream, 1990
Found wood, nails, leather, plywood, dowels,
polyurethane
21 x 17 x 6"

When I was young, my father made Miss Hickory dolls out of a hickory nut and a twig. He cut slits in the nut and inserted little splinters of wood to represent the eyes and nose. My mother read me books about vegetable people and talking trees. It should come as no surprise, then, that I like to make human heads and bodies out of wood gleaned from the forest floor and wood pile.

Throughout the world and throughout history, people have sought spirits in all types of things— cows, trees, the wind, the sea, the earth itself. Indeed, I sometimes think of the wood as holding the spirits of people frozen in time.

I think it would be wrong to remove mankind from the cycle of nature by removing whole classes of resources from human use. The decision not to use wood for furniture and housing, for example, requires the use of substitutes like plastic and aluminum, which have a far more serious potential impact on the world's ecology. Would it not be better simply to return to an earlier ethic that called for the use of resources with reverence and in moderation?

The revolution in our relationship with the earth will not simply come from curbing the activity of outside entities, such as governments, corporations, and foreign interests. The revolution must arise out of how we as individuals consume and live, as part of a world in which everything is interrelated in a complex web of life.

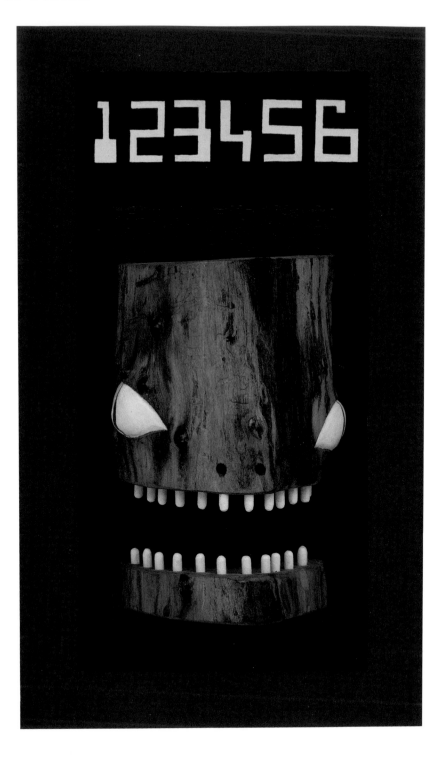

Dewey Garrett
b. 1947
Livermore, California

Serendipity, 1993
Recycled oak and padauk
4" h., 10" dia.

I visited a friend who was replacing wood strips in the water-damaged oak floor of a house undergoing restoration and was dismayed to find the discarded wood destined for the city dump. To my friend's surprise, I salvaged the cast-off material and took it to my shop. After I pulled the flooring nails and planed the material to remove the water stains, I had a good supply of 2-in.-wide, 1/4-in.-thick oak slats in random lengths.

Finding ways to use such an odd assortment of material is sometimes difficult. These turned bowls are made from thin slats glued in a lattice configuration and turned on the lathe into forms that reveal the moiré patterns in their structure. The only problem was that the slats were too narrow for the bowl size I like to make. This problem, however, created an unexpected opportunity to use scraps of 1/2-in.-square padauk cutoffs I had saved for a long time. I glued the padauk strips between the oak slats to make wider boards. The contrasting colors and textures of the woods contribute to the bowl's design, and only an occasional patched nail hole reveals the origin of the material.

A single bowl made from wood scraps presents no grand solution for forest conservation, but I hope it illustrates that conservation includes both the saving and the reuse of resources. Any saving at all is better than wasting.

Eric Gesler
b. 1958
Dana Robes Wood Craftsmen
Enfield, New Hampshire

Spare Essentials Coffee Table, 1993
Machiche, recycled mahogany
17¹/₂ x 40 x 19"
Lent by Dana Robes Wood Craftsmen

There are two aspects to conservation: preservation, or the careful management to ensure that something will last; and minimalism, the efficient use of resources.

Minimalist by design, this table uses very little material compared to standard coffee tables. A series of kerfs have been made on the underside of the table so that, in lieu of skirts, the top is held in place by a pair of battens. These same battens are employed as a base for the legs and the drawer slides. The quality of workmanship—including the dovetailed drawer joints and the through-tenoned and wedged legs—combined with engineering that anticipates seasonal wood movement guarantees that this piece will be functional for a long time.

The primary wood is machiche, a lesser-known species harvested by the Plan Piloto Forestal, a community-based project that closely manages the selective cutting of machiche and other timbers in the forests of Mexico's Yucatan peninsula. Since the project's inception in 1983, there has been a net gain in the amount of standing machiche as well as a new source of income created for remote villagers. The demand for this lesser-known species has yet to develop fully because management has had difficulty establishing dependable distribution networks and markets.

The table's drawer bottom and sides are of recycled, Bronx 2000 mahogany. In the program sponsored by Bronx 2000, discarded freight pallets are collected and either dismantled for raw lumber or repaired for resale to businesses located in the Bronx borough of New York City. Close examination of the drawer will reveal the occasional nail hole that betrays the wood's former life on the loading docks. In addition to providing an innovative new source of lumber, Bronx 2000 has created jobs and played a pivotal role in reversing the migration of business out of the Bronx.

Hank Gilpin

b. 1946
Lincoln, Rhode Island

Writing Delight, 1993
Elm, spalted elm
$29^{1}/_{8}$ x $35^{3}/_{8}$ x $17^{3}/_{4}$"

Professionally I have been somewhat ambivalent toward tropical "exotic" lumber and prefer to use domestic hardwoods for my furnituremaking. I have never felt, however, that the needs of a handful of small furniture shops scattered around the globe could have any measurable impact on the rainforests. If I might be so bold to suggest, assuming a modicum of humility, cutting a few trees for our purposes might do no harm at all.

I feel the protection of rainforests is less a matter of reducing the number of trees being cut for timber production than a question of dealing with a burgeoning world population. I can't believe that millions of acres of fores fall exclusively for glamorous, rosewood-paneled corporate boardrooms or even for simple teak cutting boards. More likely these acres of forest (each harboring very few "desirable" timber species) are cut and cleared to fulfill an overpowering and perhaps elusive demand for a higher standard of living amongst the exploding populations inhabiting the equatorial regions.

It seems that a dynamic similar to that which led to the destruction of the North American hardwood forests in the eighteenth and nineteenth centuries is working its way through the tropics. Between 1488 and 1815, the population of Europe increased from seventy-three million to over two hundred million, and the chance for a better life, the promise of land ownership, and the dream of a cornucopia led Europeans to settle and exploit our continent. Over eighty percent of the forest was cut, burned, and cleared to open land for agriculture; very little found its way to the sawmill. Industrial forces razed it to fuel railroads and iron furnaces. The forest fell prey to the

incredible zeal of the American Dream and its millions of proponents.

Perhaps it is this same American Dream infecting the less developed populations of the tropical climates that so threatens the fragile forest of Southeast Asia, South America, and Africa.

Carolyn Grew-Sheridan
b. 1947
John Grew-Sheridan
b. 1944
San Francisco, California

Reliquary, 1993
Bark, mail-order catalogues, hard maple,
Port Orford cedar, wenge, Direct Marketing
Association postcards
8 x 27 x 12"

At least fourteen million trees are cut each year in the United States to make paper for mail-order catalogues. This reliquary—an empty tree—rests on a pedestal of catalogues and holds three wooden blocks, or relics, to provoke us to contemplate the tree, its printed pulp, and the explicit mass consumerism the catalogues represent.

The woods were selected as commentary on the complex issues of timber use and deforestation:

—Hard maple from the East Coast, exported to European consumers who no longer want to use tropical hardwoods, is threatened by acid rain.

—Port Orford cedar from the Pacific Northwest has been victimized by clear-cutting, which is encouraged by unreasonable export laws and corporate greed.

—Wenge from West Africa is but one of many tropical species endangered by the exploitation of the people and resources of the Third World.

—The bark is a symbol of hope. It was found on north coast California land that was severely logged and is now being privately reforested as a nature preserve.

Overcoming inertia can be the most difficult first step in any significant project, process, or journey. Eliminating unwanted catalogues by sending in one of the postcards offered in this piece can be your first step. Small as each step may be, collectively they have an impact.

Pine Box, 1993
Pine, junk-mail "board"
10 x 22 x 8.5 cm

A living pine tree: the shared beginning of a
piece of solid pine and a pile of unnecessary
mail. Here, that junk mail is glued to form a
solid board and reunited with its relative.

Pine Box expresses some of the issues of use and
misuse of timber resources. Pine pulp farms
replace diverse forests in the name of

reforestation. Inadequate laws stipulate a paper
may be labeled as "recycled" when only ten
percent of its content is from postconsumer
waste.

We used metric measurements when designing
and making *Pine Box* as a meditation on the
necessity of thinking and working in new ways.

Kenton D. Hall

b. 1955
Muncie, Indiana

Tickticktick, 1993
Douglas fir plywood, brass and steel works
19 x 16 x 9"

Wood has always been a part of my life. As a child, I tore things apart, then either lost interest or used the parts to create something new. My maternal grandfather worked in a lumberyard and had a workshop in his basement. At a young age, I discovered the smell of wood while drilling, sawing, or burning it. My father's parents lived on a farm where I learned, unintentionally, about the structural properties of wood by crawling around in the barn. Those building skills came in handy when my cousins and I wanted to build a new fort in the woods. Later, in college, I began to use woodworking as therapy to offset the rigors of reading and writing. I also then realized that working with wood was a need and a means to express and to communicate.

Simple, practical forms and common, recycled materials describe my life's experiences, my thought processes, and how I use the objects around me. It is these aspects of my grandparents' and my parents' lives that have been passed on to me and that I now build upon.

This mantel clock displays an efficient use of Douglas fir plywood, a common domestic wood with a unique and wonderful character, harvested under controversial conditions. It is a wood from which we build our many homes, but, as a tree, it is where the spotted owl also makes its home. As the bird's fate is debated, we continue to use large quantities of this resource.

Stephen Hogbin
b. 1942
Owen Sound, Ontario, Canada

Buttoning Wood, 1993
Chacahuante, fir, medium-density fiberboard,
paint
5 x 23 x 19"

Buttoning Wood is part of a series I have been working on that refers to mending, restoration, repair, revival, and renewal. I have been interested in images that are metaphorical or mediate concerns for the environment. *Buttoning Wood* demonstrates the progress of stasis. Standing still—being rooted in place—is fundamental to understanding conservation.

Buttoning Wood is centered on an axis; the form is symmetrical, an easy form to comprehend. The disparity of materials, altered surfaces of the wood, and the inclusion of text create discomfort and an interest in the proposition of buttoning and place. To sew something up is to finish something; to button into place, to buttonhole the subject.

The needle, button, and fabric have no thread, which requires the viewer to sew an imagined thread through the subject. Conservation by design demands an ability to thread together not only things, but also concepts.

Richard Hooper
b. 1958
Liverpool, Merseyside, England

Birch Plywood Bowl, 1992
Laminated birch plywood, PVA glue
7" h., 14" dia.

The visual and structural properties of wood offer the maker the opportunity to create forms that are quite distinct from those of other materials, such as ceramics or metal. These unique properties are manifest even in the humblest species of wood.

The interplay of simple, solid forms in this bowl is accentuated by strata of laminated birch plywood (widely available from sustainably managed sources). I often stain the laminates black to add visual weight to the piece and to suggest neoprimitive, neoclassical, or postapocalyptic forms.

Michael Hosaluk

b. 1954
Saskatoon, Saskatchewan, Canada

Traveling Bowl—Australia, 1993
Elm, paint, hair, dye
15½ x 10¾ x 7"
Lent by Robyn Hutcheson Horn

Someone once said to me, "There's no good wood in Saskatchewan." I took that as a challenge and, for the last ten years, I have used wood from our province in most of my work.

The source of the material has been varied: leftovers at logging sites, trees cut down by city crews or private tree cutters, remnants at garbage dumps or salvage yards. I have found incredible logs and burls of birch, poplar, maple, elm, ash, mahogany lumber, oak, pine, various fruit woods, and shrubs too numerous to mention. Most of it was free or purchased at minimal cost.

The processes of finding the material and then making the first chainsaw cuts, to expose woods as exotic as any species in the world, give me a greater reverence for my material and for the work I produce from it.

I found the wood for *Traveling Bowl* while on a walk in Australia. It tells stories of my travels in that country. The wood was a three-dimensional canvas to portray my ideas. The focus is the structure of the wood, not the grain. Our ideas are what count, and, if they are strong, they will communicate, regardless of the material.

Dwight N. Huffman
b. 1966
John Rantanen
b. 1961
Haute House
Ithaca, New York

Furniture For Recyclables: Butcher Block Bin Table, 1992
Maple, Livos finish
51 x 25³/₄ x 36³/₄"

As America nears the next millenium, perhaps no problem is as immediate as that of waste disposal. Part of the solution is recycling.

What contribution can artists make? We can render recycling beautiful. Artists determine popular culture. If our designs appeal to those with aesthetic sensibilities, they will eventually appeal to everybody.

Through our work, we wish to integrate recycling into everyday life and space. Our design principle is to make furniture that serves multiple functions. Our pieces are intended to meet the difficult demands of tight living quarters by making use of otherwise wasted space, such as corners or the area underneath open counters. We use local hardwoods exclusively for construction.

We use wood glue conservatively, if at all, and the most environmentally friendly finish we can find.

Although our designs function as a practical way of storing recyclables, we strive to transform the mundane into art. Our vehicle is pattern. Our patterns soothe. They are intended, through the blending of art with the ordinary, to assist people as they adapt to a new world of which recycling is an integral part.

Dean Johnston
b. 1956
Kahului, Hawaii

Furniture As American Pastime, Q.M.1, 1993
Queensland maple, recycled baseball
bats, paint
28 x 17 x 17"

Life on a relatively small island with its own precious and vulnerable ecosystem offers a clear and cutting insight into the interconnectedness of the earth's species.

The seat for this stool is made of Queensland maple, a smooth-grained, medium-density hardwood. Queensland maple has been planted in Hawaii throughout the last fifty years in an effort to provide woodworkers with a sustainable supply of quality hardwood. The legs and stretchers are made from used baseball bats, picked out of garage sales and Salvation Army thrift stores. Because most of the work for the stool was done on the drill press, its construction consumed very little energy.

The top of the seat features an airbrushed *trompe l'oeil* version of a baseball, a response to one of my personal "beefs"—cattle and our insatiable appetite for hamburgers are the true culprits of deforestation. By creating a faux-leather seat, I hope to save a cow from needing to be born.

This piece invites artists, designers, and consumers to draw from a broad palette of materials and technologies to create objects of lasting worth with a minimal impact on the earth.

The wood was purchased from Winkler Wood Products (261-A Kekuanaoa Street, Hilo, HI 96720). Ed Winkler is in the process of sawing and drying a large number of lesser-known and lesser-used local species that will be made available to wood artists for the show "Woods of Hawaii '93 The 10% Challenge." The show's criteria include the use of Hawaii's sustainable lesser-known species and not more than ten percent of endangered woods.

Thomas Kamila
b. 1950
Ashburnham, Massachusetts

Ice Fall, 1992
Red oak, filler, lacquer
13¹/₂" h., 9" dia.
Illustrated

China Blue, 1992
Red oak, filler, lacquer
7" h., 10" dia.

I have been asked many times, "Why do you turn red oak? It's such a common wood." The question recalls the memory of a young boy sitting on an oak stair tread, studying the erosive patterns etched in its surface by a thousand trips to the basement of my childhood home.

This old image is at the heart of my most recent woodturning. The grain patterns produced on the surface of my red oak vessels fascinate me—such a lovely secret hidden just beneath the surface of such a common wood. By using the pith of the tree for the turning axis, the annual growth rings become a rhythmic dance. These patterns are evidence of the tree's silent witness to years long past. Each passing year is one more stroke of God's pen.

It is natural for human beings, and especially artists, to see the beauty that surrounds us. Working with wood, I haven't had to look very far. I will continue to use what is naturally at hand for my material and inspiration.

Silas Kopf

b. 1949
Northampton, Massachusetts

Writing Desk, 1992
Walnut, maple, bog oak, EBON-X, tagua nut
30 x 64 x 26"

The walnut "oysters" that form the borders of the writing desk were made from the limbs of a local tree, which blew over in a hurricane that passed through New England in August 1991.

The small diameter of the material made it useful for little more than firewood. Oysters were sometimes used on English furniture during the eighteenth century, but they are difficult to cut and dry. My intent was to make a backyard material "exotic" and to show that such a material could be used in a unique, decorative manner.

The bog oak that forms the writing surface is another "exotic" wood. The tree died long ago and was submerged in a bog, where the water

reacted with the tannic acid in the wood to turn it a charcoal color. Bog oak was also used for decorative effect in antique woodwork.

EBON-X is a chemically treated walnut, which can be used as an ebony substitute for black details in furniture. Tagua nut is a sustainable tropical-forest product, which can likewise be used as an ivory substitute.

Peter Kovacsy
b. 1953
Pemberton, Western Australia, Australia

Emotion #4:
Don't Let Me Get Too Deep, 1993
Sheoak, medium-density fiberboard, brass,
foil, shellac, tung oil, beeswax, casein paint,
lacquer
3^{15}/$_{16}$" h., 15^{1}/$_{2}$" dia.

In my *Emotion* series, I approach the use of
native timbers with the aim of maximizing the
number of pieces I can make from a single
piece of wood. To achieve this, I have
introduced composite manufactured material
for the structural body. The technical
properties of sheoak, which is native to
Western Australia, limit its tendency to shrink
or warp and make it ideally suited for use in this
type of composite construction.

Keith Kutch

b. 1948
Savannah, Georgia

Etruscan Throne Paradox, 1993
Recycled plastic, galvanized steel, rosewood veneer
32 x 30 x 20"

Why do we demand that our furniture be made of exotic woods from endangered areas? What created the assumption that Brazilian rosewood, for example, is intrinsically more beautiful than some other more commonly available material?

I submit that it is no more than tradition and habit. The aristocracy and privileged classes have always demanded that their possessions be made of the rarest and most expensive materials—not because they were any more beautiful than more accessible woods, but because they enhanced the owner's status.

To ameliorate the situation of the rainforests, it is not enough to use temperate woods only. This will not resolve the issue. We must re-educate ourselves and challenge our assumptions about the use of rare and exotic materials. Certainly, a piece of ebony, rosewood, or curly maple is beautiful, but no more so than phenolic resin, steel, or recycled polypropylene. We must learn to appreciate the intrinsic beauty of all materials if we are to utilize efficiently the material we have on hand—wisely used rainforest woods as well as alternative materials.

The design of this chair is loosely based on that of an Etruscan throne, dating from about 600 B.C. The original was made of bronze, a particularly expensive material in its time. For the vertical structural elements, I used sheets of recycled plastic, manufactured from discarded containers. For the seat and as the main horizontal support structure, I used corrugated galvanized sheet steel, which I veneered with a discarded rosewood sample. I attempted to use these materials in a way that expresses their functional and structural natures as well as their particular beauty.

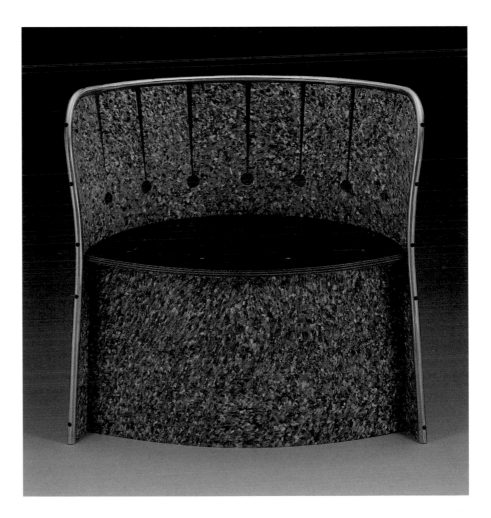

William Laskin
b. 1953
Toronto, Ontario, Canada

I Have Three Things To Say, 1993
Maple, Plexiglas, paper, Spanish cedar, steel
bolts, steel strings, inlays of mother-of-pearl,
gold mother-of-pearl, Tahitian black shell,
abalone, alloy gold, alloy silver, bone, burled
maple, ebony, wax engraving filler
43 x 36 x 28"

Within the luthier's trade, experimenting with
sustainably harvested tropical species and
plentiful domestic woods—even modern
synthetics—is an ongoing occurrence. We
search not only for "good" woods, but for
underutilized varieties that can deliver the
required tonal qualities. As this sculpture took
shape, it grew to concern itself with three
distinct but interrelated issues.

1. I transform pieces of trees into a sonorous
object by shaping, refining, and manipulating
the material. In the process, how easy it is to
lose sight of the original tree, of its beauty
and intrinsic value, and of the fact that,
without it, most instrument makers would be
doing something less with their lives.

   Thus, the guitar neck grows directly out of a
raw stump of Ontario maple. The haphazard
locations of the strings, which converge
toward order on their way to the peghead,
also mimic nature's randomness. The ugly,
oversized bolts—stand-ins for the 1-in. pins
that normally anchor guitar strings in the
top—represent invasive technologies, the
tools by which we achieve our ends.

2. Within my lifetime, ebony may become too
rare to remain a commercial timber. This
dense and elegant wood, the traditional
fingerboard material for stringed instruments,
is being depleted by overharvesting. My
portrait of four guitar makers, inlaid and
engraved into the guitar neck, provides a
cross section of reactions to this critical
event. On the left I am feebly attempting to

prevent the ebony fingerboard from dripping
away. I try to retrieve it, my efforts amount
to a proverbial drop in the bucket. My watch
shows five minutes to midnight. To my right,
Sergei de Jonge evinces shock at the scenario.
Next to him stands Linda Manzer, confronting
you-the-viewer, for we all play a role in this
process, whether instrument maker, musician,
or listening public. Last is David Wren,
resigned but downcast, accepting, if he must,
the loss of such a precious material.

3. The act of pulling music from wood exacts a
"blood" price. In order to satisfy the human
desire for pleasing sounds, for tones capable
of shifting our emotions like the moon and
the ocean's tides, trees die. Instrument
makers recognize the potential for music
beneath the bark, but they must also remain
aware that a once-living organism is the
provider. Lose that awareness and we lose
the reverence for—and the careful use of—
the substance upon which we depend.

Lucinda Leech

b. 1954
Oxford, Oxfordshire, England

Chair, 1993
Vitex, chontaquiro, oil finish
47 x 32 x 24"

The vitex for this chair came from Iumi Tugetha Holdings in the Solomon Islands. Iumi buys timber from a variety of small-scale operations run by customary landowners, such as Everest Ega, who cuts vitex in the Aruligo area on the western side of Guadalcanal. Ega and his relatives use a chainsaw mill, which allows the timber to be processed where it falls. Small clearings are created throughout the forest, which regenerate naturally, just as traditional garden plots have always done. Ega's group is working towards developing an "Eco-Forest Management Plan" with the help of Soltrust, a nongovernmental organization that evolved from the Foundation for the People of the South Pacific. Forestry specialists have commended their work and recommend they be encouraged through trade to continue and complete the process.

The vitex tree is gnarled and twisted and covered in vines and creepers. Its local name in the Solomons is *fassa,* and in neighboring Papua New Guinea, where it is traditionally used for drums and canoes, it is known as *garamut.* Increasingly, it is used for carving. Vitex is quite common in the outer islands, but has not been much exported. As with many native species elsewhere, there is now a ban on log exports in the Solomon Islands; milling provides added value for the country of origin.

The four turned bars in the back of the chair are made from chontaquiro (*Diplotropis martiusil*), from the Yanesha Cooperative in Central Peru, chosen for its contrasting color and texture.

I designed the chair after seeing the timber, which had been milled in large slabs, reflecting the simplicity of the available technology in the forest. This led me to create a "chunky" design, reducing needless reprocessing. The curves are intended to echo the organic shape of the tree, and the size and weight will perhaps remind the viewer of the qualities of the wood in its original form. The chair is intended for outdoor use to exploit vitex's excellent durability.

Thomas Loeser
b. 1956
Madison, Wisconsin

Cardboard Box, 1990
Corrugated cardboard, colored paper
15 x 23¹/₄ x 14"

I became interested in cardboard as a cheap, not-too-attractive material. I planned to create a "trial separation" from the precious and seductive qualities of the natural wood and painted surfaces that I love and use in most of my work. Part of the appeal of cardboard was that I could work quickly and experimentally without worrying about mistakes. From a box-manufacturing company, I got a free

pickup-truck load of corrugated cardboard that was going to be discarded because it had been cut to the wrong size. In its single-sheet thickness, the material conjured images of flimsy boxes. To get away from that familiar visual reference, I glued up large blocks of cardboard in a veneer press and then remilled it into workable thicknesses by bandsawing at various angles. In effect, I was remanufacturing the raw materials for my projects by making cardboard "lumber." The most unexpected discovery was that, despite my original intentions, the material turned out to be inherently beautiful.

For *Cardboard Box*, I glued up corrugated paper with colored paper laminated between each layer and then joined the resawn slabs with

dovetails. Because dovetails are considered such a classic and enduring form of joinery, they create some interesting contradictions when used with impermanent materials like paper and cardboard. Despite my best efforts, this piece will probably self-destruct in a matter of years, rather than the decades or centuries implied by the joinery. While it survives, I hope it raises some questions about man-made versus natural materials, about which materials possess desirable aesthetic qualities and, in the end, about what we consider worthless and what precious.

Kristina Madsen
b. 1955
Easthampton, Massachusetts

Bench, 1993
Maple, wenge, ebony
13 x 50 x 11"

I am an admirer and user of tropical woods and I maintain that selectively harvested forests offer a valuable, renewable resource. As yet, there are few sources of certified, well-managed lumber or lesser-known species. The small-scale operations that are now trying to harvest selectively lack accurate drying data for lesser-known species. The wood that they ship to this country is often less than furniture grade.

Because of the difficulty in obtaining seasoned, certified wood, I selected well-known species from my own stock, acknowledging their rarity and employing them sparingly.

The strain on the rainforest results from far more than destructive forestry practices, but poverty, overpopulation, and the need for agricultural land are not issues that we foreign small fry can greatly affect. As furnituremakers, however, we can encourage ecologically sound forestry practices by supporting sustainable sources. We can also help make good management ecologically viable by compensating the indigenous peoples well for their effort and for their trees.

As part of my contribution to this exhibition, I will donate the income from the sale of my bench to establish a WARP fund in aid and support of forestry projects that are striving to harvest sustainably. I hope that this fund will grow large enough that we can facilitate certification, develop drying technology, supply equipment and training, and otherwise help rainforest communities to profit from and maintain the health of their forests.

John Makepeace
b. 1939
Beaminster, Dorset, England

Phoenix II, 1993
Holly, burr elm, bog oak
68 x 34 x 21"

This chair draws its name from the mythological bird—the only one of its kind—that, after living for five or six centuries in the Arabian desert, burnt itself on its own funeral pyre, then rose from the ashes with renewed youth to live through another cycle.

Such myths of nature's capacity to survive have always been deeply rooted in the cultural psyche. But now for the first time the increasing rate of environmental change is evident within a single generation. Confronted by the threat of the future extinction of our species, the need for conservation becomes a sharper reality.

Made from discarded natural materials, most commonly used as firewood, the timbers in this chair celebrate a rich diversity:

—The fine white holly, evocative of fresh growth, was once used for inlays and for wedges to split logs. No one seems to want it now, but it burns well.

—Largely bereft of elm trees since the advent of Dutch elm disease, coffins are now made of chipboard. Burr elm was never popular in this market. Occasionally, a turner might seek it out, but its unpredictable character and defects are unacceptable to most furnituremakers.

—The black bog oak, buried these five thousand years since the tree was blown over in a hurricane, has been preserved in sodden peat, its color resulting from the reaction between the tannin in the oak and the alkaline soil. Such trees are unearthed by farmers' plows and provide fuel for the next winter.

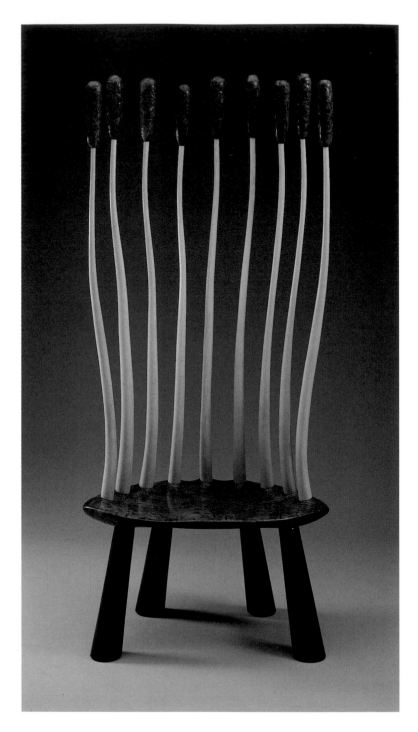

John Marcoux
b. 1922
Providence, Rhode Island

Made In The U.S.A., 1992
Basswood, stainless steel, glass shelves,
lacquer, interior lighting
72 x 23 x 16"

Modern furniture designers, like industrial
designers, can achieve beautiful design through
engineering. There are stunning, early examples
of this, such as the designs of Michael Thonet,
which also combine ornamentation with
conservation. Thonet developed new
engineering techniques for his bentwood
designs, using scaled-down components and
beech, a locally available wood with a reputation
for utility.

The basswood in *Made in The U.S.A.* is a fast-
growing, easily renewable resource with a
reputation for good tensile strength, stability
when properly dried, and little or no visible
grain pattern. (For these reasons, it makes
excellent yardsticks and is a valuable building
material.) The ¹/₈-in.-thick skin of *Made in The
U.S.A.* is reinforced structurally in a zigzag
configuration. I made the stainless-steel
hardware, finished it carefully, and left it
exposed as part of the design.

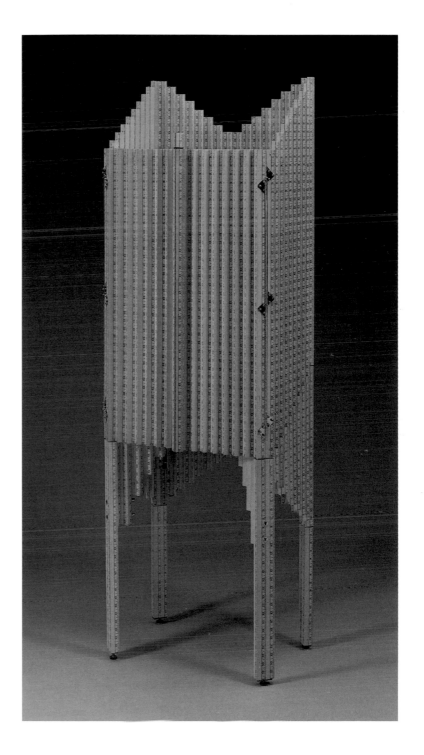

Wendy Maruyama

b. 1952
(Christine Lowe, metalwork)
San Diego, California

Candelabrum, 1993
Carved and polychromed jelutong,
electroplated copper
84 x 38 x 28"

My recent work has been inspired by fantasy.
The furniture has the organic and fluid sensibility
of natural botanical forms in a style I would dub
"romantic rococo."

With this piece, I tried to imagine what it might
be like in a tropical forest, where the wood I
used came from, and then to visually recreate
it—although I acknowledge that it may be a
twisted notion, not unlike taxidermy, to remove
a living thing from the forest and then try to
reconstruct it and its relationship to that
environment.

The candle symbolizes this romantic ideal in the
way it throws off light and creates dancing
shadows. In combination with the florid colors
and forms, the light brings the impression of the
outdoors into an interior space.

Alphonse Mattia

b. 1947
Westport, Massachusetts

Pencil Ascending, 1993
Curly maple, walnut, poplar, Douglas fir,
chipboard, Baltic plywood, delrin, mirror
57³/₄ x 30¹/₂ x 9¹/₄"

"SO...
Catch!" calls the Once-ler.
He lets something fall.
"It's a Truffula Seed.
It's the last one of all!
You're in charge of the last of the
Truffula Seeds. And Truffula Trees are what
   everyone needs.
Plant a new Truffula. Treat it with care.
Give it clean water.
And feed it fresh air.
Grow a forest. Protect it from axes that hack.
Then the Lorax and all of his friends may come
   back."
                              —Dr. Seuss, *The Lorax*

I have been trying to de-emphasize the
importance of precious materials in my
work, although there is no getting around the
appeal of the scarce and the exotic. I get a
lot of satisfaction from conserving and
protecting our resources by choosing more
common and renewable woods. I hope this
exhibition will introduce us to some novel
approaches to materials and help to increase
our understanding and acceptance of objects
that do not rely so heavily on the use of
endangered timbers.

Peter Murkett

b. 1946
Monterey, Massachusetts

Salvage Chair, 1993
Recycled red maple and red oak, steel strapping
42¹/₂ x 22¹/₂ x 18¹/₂"

And you, my father, there on the sad height,
Curse, bless, me now with your fierce tears,
    I pray,
Do not go gentle into that good night.
Rage, rage against the dying of the light.
                    —Dylan Thomas, "Do Not Go Gentle
                            Into That Good Night"

Recycling, conservation, control of pollution and population all make compelling good sense as ways of fixing the mess we have made. They are things we can, must, will do—the rational aspect.

Salvage Chair is a post-and-rung armchair made of woods selected from a few used pallets. The seat is woven of used steel binding straps. This is an angular, bony, cracked, and crooked chair, riddled with nail holes and saw-marked surfaces. It is a fitting throne for the masters of the universe. The steel seat is cold.

The crisis is large, and the hour is late. We may well fail to save ourselves and trees. We may have failed already. We should sit down and shut up. We are not the world.

Yet, if we have used up the incomparable Caribbean mahogany (*Swietenia mahagoni*), still we can reuse what scraps we have left, and make them over into something durable, with a suitably awkward beauty.

Christoph Neander

b. 1959
Providence, Rhode Island

Soothing The Blues, 1993
Eastern white pine (affected by fungus),
maple, cedar, acrylic paint, fabric, pastel chalk,
beeswax
21 1/2 x 42 x 20"

When we look at precious woods—tropical hardwoods and rare native species—we experience warmth from the pleasing colors, excitement from the bold patterns and contrasts. The imaginative use of native species can evoke these same feelings.

Pine—colorful, abundant, full of worth, yet so often ignored. This blanket chest explores the range of aesthetic possibilities in a commonplace raw material. Ideals of beauty are not so much an objective truth as a conditioned response. When artists challenge the viewer with new standards of beauty, a learning process begins.

I used pine sapwood stained by a fungus growth from improper drying, which would normally downgrade this otherwise attractive wood. Grey-blue "discolorations" permeate the grain without causing structural damage. Fields and dashes of grey-blue stain flow gently along the curved surfaces and throughout the grain of the wood. They appear as bold, natural brush

strokes of watercolor to complement the pine's familiar warmth. Bright accents of paint, softened by a mottled texture, lie just below the surface, providing depth and definition of shape.

The oriental plainness of this chest is also meant to evoke a sense of simplicity, which I believe we need to introduce in our lives to achieve a balance with the natural environment.

In my native Germany, skilled craftspersons build expensive furniture from native softwoods in ways that have yet to be embraced by American artisans and consumers. From the design and execution of these pieces come a different kind of beauty and a sense of enduring value.

Robert O'Neal
b. 1939
Rehoboth, Massachusetts

Foresthope, 1993
Wood, paper, paper pulp with glass beads,
rattan, recycled vacuum-cleaner brush
50 x 42 x 32"

This piece represents a seedpod as a container,
and symbolizes a fresh start, a new beginning in
using the resources that nature can provide
without exploiting or endangering the
environment. The pod or chest configuration is
ideal for housing articles of clothing made from
natural fibers by allowing more casual care and
maintenance in folding and storing these articles.

It is exciting to work with a new and diverse
range of natural materials that help conserve
and extend special and rare woods. The first
inspiration for this project was a concern for
material. But the vision soon expanded to
embrace the richness of design possibilities and
an intensified appreciation for the direct and
diverse ways natural materials can and should be
used—and the ways they have traditionally been
used by people and cultures with limited
resources. There's no longer a difference
between underdeveloped and overdeveloped
countries in the need to rely on conserved
resources to express beauty, find comfort, and
create variety.

This piece is dedicated to the spirits of all those
who have had a part in bringing it to life.

Timothy Philbrick

b. 1952
Narragansett, Rhode Island

Lamp Stand, 1993
Pau ferro, marble
32 x 17 x 12"

The pau ferro used to make this table is from old stock, probably from Brazil. I'm told that much of the pau ferro shipped from Brazil comes from logs smuggled across the border from Bolivia. Unfortunately, the middlemen who sell the lumber will tell buyers what they think they want to hear. It's often impossible to identify the origin of the lumber, and what one is told is unverifiable. Perhaps the more we ask, the more the truth will find its way out.

Given the value and scarcity of this lovely wood, I have designed a small piece that consumes a minimum of lumber. The top is Negro Marquino marble, a material that may be being replenished in the Earth's crust at this moment.

Tom Rauschke
b. 1950
Kaaren Wiken
b. 1948
Palmyra, Wisconsin

Forest Fire Bowls, 1993
Hickory, fiber
11½" h., 8¾" dia.
Private collection

Made primarily from native American
hardwoods, our work focuses on the small
niches and natural places in our world, and
presents each as a sacred place, worthy of
reverence. We convey the awe and appreciation
inspired by the larger world that our pieces
represent, and from which the materials for our
work come. Once it was a tree, now it is
The Forest.

The wooden shapes are turned on a lathe,
then cut, carved, and altered to become unique
landscapes and environments. Integrated into
these dioramas are Kaaren's embroideries of
local inhabitants and points of interest.
The miniature embroideries add color and life
to the pieces and can often be removed to be
worn as jewelry.

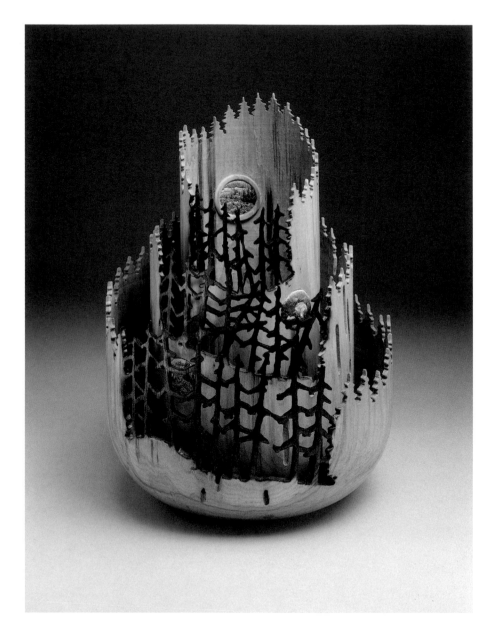

Photo by Cathy Carver.

Christopher Rose

b. 1950
Brighton, East Sussex, England

Garden Chair, 1993
Vitex, bronze
25 x 17 x 17"

This simple garden chair utilizes an elementary design and only one type of woodworking joint. It is one of the companions to an existing garden table. The folding chair back was designed for compactness and to avoid complicated woodwork. When not in use, the chair may be tucked beneath the table to protect the seat.

Rainforests in Papua New Guinea have increasingly been the victims of gross exploitation. Vitex is one of several lesser-known species marketed by the Ecological Trading Company (ETC) from Masurina Limited in Milne Bay Province, Papua New Guinea. (Certification and specifier's information is available through the ETC.)

Vitex is durable and able to withstand fifteen to twenty years of unprotected contact with the ground. It is nonsiliceous, good for heavy construction, exterior joinery, and the building of boats, wharves, decking, stair treads, and garden furniture. It machines well, is suitable for bending, and seasons without degrading. It is comparable to afrormosia and teak.

It is said that to know a name is to have power over the person or object. We are going to encounter many new names such, such as vitex, in our effort to use lesser-known species. Many of our associations and notions of quality are connected to an old order of attitudes. Good design may help develop markets for new materials while providing some breathing space for older species.

Mitch Ryerson
b. 1955
Cambridge, Massachusetts

Milk Crate Table, 1993
Plastic milk crate, wood, glass, milk cartons,
milk-jug caps
29$^{1}/_{2}$ x 14 x 14"

I decided to make a piece of furniture by
recycling a familiar, commonplace object—a milk
crate—and, in the process, to display the crate's
inherent value in an unexpected way. I like using
found objects and common materials. It's what
we do with them that makes them valuable.

Paul Sasso
b. 1948
Almo, Kentucky

We Barely Know Her, 1993
Poplar, basswood, bird's-eye maple,
acrylic paint
52 x 22 x 11"

I have never known a person interested in
beauty to destroy *anything* without careful
consideration. Our world's environmental
problems are directly related to an aesthetic
deficit. That is why art is so important.

Kenneth Scherdell

b. 1957
Worcester, Massachusetts

Barnborn, 1993
Weathered, recycled oak
19 x 46¹/₄ x 17"

A friend's old shed held a few lengths of barn board destined for the wood stove. Rather than recycle them into the atmosphere, and because my house was due for a paint job, we decided the boards would make useful staging planks and moved them to my wood pile.

After I had finished a series of fussy, meticulous pieces, I needed to loosen up. Those weathered oak planks held some promise as I pondered creating a bench that would retain the essence of their rough-sawn, grey surface and yet be refined enough to be used as furniture. The design had to be fun, functional, spontaneous, and not consume a huge amount of time. I wanted to introduce an element of asymmetry to my work and to leave the marks of the maker, which are evident in the scribed lines and hand-planed texture.

I have yet to paint the house.

Lee Schuette
b. 1951
Kittery Point, Maine

Hi-Tech Shaker Chair: Mama, 1993
Plantation-grown teak, salvaged aluminum,
black chrome bolts, cotton tape
42 x 20 x 18"

The Shakers lived simply, economically, and honestly. I have studied the Shaker ladderback chair as an object that truly expresses these values. The chairs in this series are not Shaker reproductions—I doubt that it's possible to improve upon the Shaker post-and-rung chair— but they are stucturally sound chairs of classical proportions, and they use only four board feet of lumber. The geometry and proportions have been altered considerably to accommodate larger bodies and more grandiose lifestyles than the Shakers could have imagined.

These chairs were designed to be shipped in a compact container and assembled by the client. The materials will withstand the elements. All of the aluminum was purchased from salvage bins; the fastenings and fabric are new.

Making the work was fun and relatively straightforward. But finding honest, accountable sources for dimensionally cut exotic hardwood was a long and bumpy road. As I shopped for wood, I went to dealers I knew and with whom I had a long-standing relationship. I told them I was looking for environmentally appropriate wood that would be good for interior and exterior applications. They suggested plantation-grown teak and purpleheart, a lesser-known yet durable hardwood.

I purchased the purpleheart, designed and built the chair and, two days before the entry deadline for this exhibition, I attempted to validate the sources. Neither of the dealers whom I had specifically asked for environmentally appropriate products could document the pathway by which these materials were cut and delivered.

This experience is all too common—dealers telling their customers what they want to hear. "Getting honest" is the most important part of the journey to appropriate management of natural resources.

[Schuette made the chair in the exhibition and catalogue out of plantation-grown teak, which he was able to locate after submitting his original design. —Ed.]

Mark Sfirri
b. 1952
New Hope, Pennsylvania

Shaky Candlesticks, 1992
Cherry
13 x 4 x 4" and 9 x 4 x 4"
Lent by Dr. Dotty Gerstley

About four years ago, when I heard a rumor about a ban on the import of wenge, I went out and bought several hundred feet of it. I thought that stockpiling for future use was a good idea. But, as I've become aware of the environmental effect of my wood choices, I have made substantial changes in my selection of species. I am exploring lesser-known tropical woods, but also have a renewed interest in the less-utilized, native woods that I haven't used in years, such as elm, box elder, and hickory. I've planted at least thirty-five trees in the last ten years, and the wenge still sits in my shop.

By designing smaller projects, I have been able to use small chunks of perfectly good wood that I would have previously considered scrap. *Shaky Candlesticks* are made of cherry that was locally grown, sawn, and dried. The title places the emphasis not on the work itself, but on the support beneath it. An ordinarily static object becomes animated with the fear that all is not well in the world.

John Shipstad
b. 1954
Coos Bay, Oregon

Wine Cabinet, 1993
Kamarere, sucupira, chontaquiro, bayo, chakte koc, madrone, plywood
32 x 31¹/₄ x 19"

The outer cabinet is made entirely from lesser-known species from recognized well-managed sources. The panels are veneered with sucupira, a lesser-known species of which the harvester is unknown (the purchase benefited WARP's 1992 fundraising sale). The frame on the back panel is chontaquiro. This is the same species as the sucupira veneer, but grown in another bioregion, which illustrates the variations in woods depending on their source. The interior wood, madrone, symbolizes our own undervaluation of species in the Pacific Northwest, where such woods are either left for scrap, chipped for fiber, or sold as firewood.

In 1988, after watching perhaps the fourth television show in three months on world deforestation, I finally realized that although our trade has deep-rooted traditions and a reverence for wood, our knowledge of and concern for the forests from which these woods are harvested are sadly lacking. As my awareness grew, so did my desire to find a solution that would allow me to practice my craft with a clear conscience.

This began an interesting, and intense, journey in the exploration of forest issues, which led eventually to a group of like-minded woodworkers and the creation of WARP. From its beginning, WARP's mission has been to supply the woodworking industry with reliable information about sources of well-managed woods, strategies for wood conservation, and the promotion of sustainable development.

Human endeavors often remove us from nature and our economic engine rarely includes ecosystem management. As a great society, we must learn land stewardship or, in just a couple of generations, pay a huge price for ignoring it.

This exhibition gives me great hope that we can turn sustainable forestry from a current trend into an industry standard.

Sources of Supply:

Part	Species	U.S. Source	Harvester	Country
Frame	Kamarere	EcoTimber	Ulatawa Estates	Papua New Guinea
Panel	Sucupira	WARP veneer sale	Unknown	Brazil
Back frame	Chontaquiro	Self	Yanesha Coop	Peru
Inlay	Bayo	Wildwoods	Plan Piloto	Mexico
Handles	Chakte koc	Wildwoods	Plan Piloto	Mexico
Interior	Madrone	Winchester Forest Products	Winchester Forest Products	Oregon
Hidden woods	Various	Shop scrap	Unknown	Unknown
Substrate	Apple plywood (maple/alder)	States Industry	Unknown	Oregon

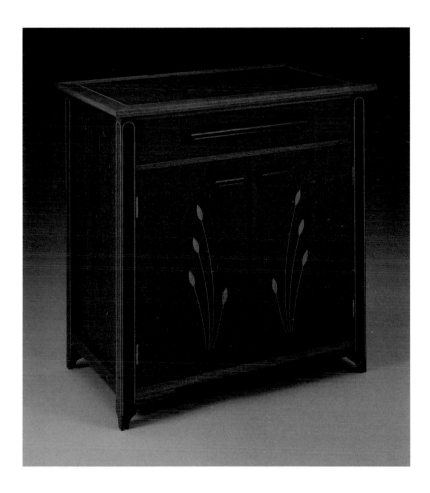

Randy Shull
b. 1962
Asheville, North Carolina

Time Sage, 1992
Logging salvage, paint
72 x 12 x 10"
Lent by courtesy of Snyderman Gallery,
Philadelphia, Pennsylvania

I have been salvaging broken tree parts for six years. They are abundant in the rural Southern mountains where I live, as logging sites throughout the region are filled with broken, splintered debris left behind by lumbermen in the name of economic growth. Also, Nature's violent storms twist and tangle trees and leave an endless variety of splintered shapes in their wake.

Finding and using these splintered shards, which would otherwise be burned, hauled off to a landfill, or left to rot, gives me great satisfaction. In these broken remnants, I find raw tension, emotion, ambiguity, strength, and beauty. It is an act of resurrection, an attempt to revive the powerful spirit of the twisted tree. I try to invoke this spirit in a way that inspires and provokes thought about the vulnerability of nature and its tenuous balance with man. Our survival and the preservation of nature rely upon our interdependency.

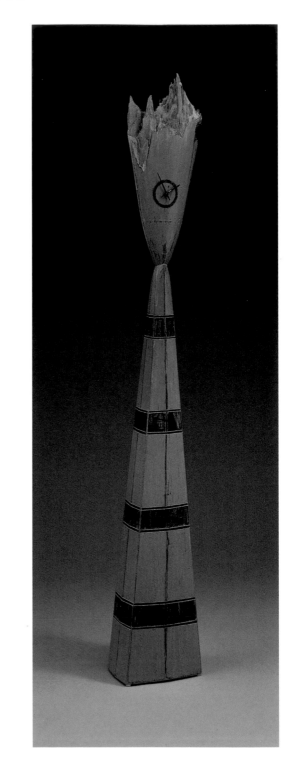

Naomi Siegmann
b. 1933
Mexico City, Mexico

Renaissance, 1993
Recycled child's chair, pine, hedge branches,
veneer, bark paper, acrylic paint
30³/₄ x 15³/₄ x 15"

Upon rediscovering my childrens' old, painted
chair, which had been around the house for at
least twenty years, I had a most delightful,
whimsical thought: an old wooden chair sits
around for so long that it actually takes root and
begins to grow again. *Renaissance* is the result.

I carved the cedar flowerpot in 1979 for a
series of pots and plants I did for my exhibition
at the Museo de Arte Moderno in Mexico City.
This particular pot was not used. (Perhaps, like
the chair, it was waiting to be regenerated.)
The dried branches growing out of the cedar
flowerpot are from a hedge in my garden; the
leaves are cut from wood veneer and amate.
(Amate is made from tree bark that is cut from
the trunk without harming the tree. The bark is
pounded into a thin, paperlike sheet and is
utilized for painting and other artistic uses.
This pre-Hispanic technique is many centuries
old and still in use today.)

The forces of nature, the greatest recycler,
show us that if we wish to endure we must
learn to respect all the elements of our
environment in our protective "household."
We must learn and care enough to replant our
forests, reuse metals and plastics, use safe
chemicals. And we must readjust our thinking
and our lives to sustain what is left of the
environment that spawned us. The alternative is
unthinkable—no more wood, no more
woodworkers, no more baby chairs, no more
babies. The true cycle of nature is to reclaim
what is rightfully hers.

Ron Smith
b. 1950
Falmouth, Massachusetts

The Essentials Of Good Grooming, 1993
Painted poplar, found objects, woven
cotton tape
54 x 32 x 28"

Materials are the tools that help us as visual
artists to tell a story, define ideas, and express
the character of our work and ourselves.
What does it say about this process if we visit
our drawing boards contemplating a list of rare
and precious materials? What does it say about
us as designers if we overutilize these resources,
making the uncommon common, projecting a
false sense of wealth?

Richness should come from ideas. The most
common woods and everyday objects can
become precious if given a new context, a new
life, a new history. When our ideas are
compatibly combined with carefully selected
materials, the final statement is rare and
valuable.

My furniture and art have become less
concerned with wood and more with collecting.
The process of collecting helps me make the
statement or define the story. I select objects
for a variety of reasons, including their color,
form, material, history, and inherent ability to
enhance my message. Like the found objects I
seek out, my wood inventory consists of
domestic, humble varieties. Wood is the
connecting medium for the objects, occasionally
selected for the surface effect it contributes to
the piece. An expensive or exotic material,
selected for only that reason, can detract from
an idea about real life.

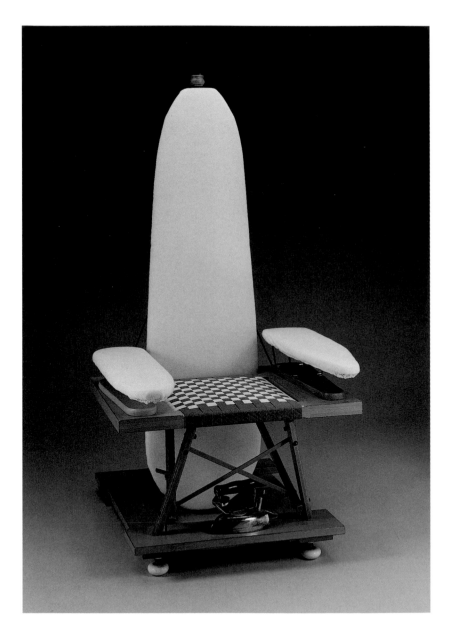

Rosanne Somerson
b. 1954
Westport, Massachusetts

Earthly Delights, 1992
Cherry, tinted maple
17 x 70 x 28"

The idea for this table grew out of my desire to bring the feeling and beauty of an exterior garden into a domestic environment. The leg forms are derived directly from the leaves and organic shapes above them, extending the organic quality in three dimensions. The leaves were positioned to suggest gesturing hands and to symbolize a cooperative spirit between the interior and natural environments. That spirit helps us define ourselves as a culture looking for meaning within a larger global community. Including this imagery in a piece that is part of the "interior landscape" will perhaps encourage us to think about the relevance of the exterior landscape to our lives every day.

The quarter-sawn cherry (chosen for its even grain and soft quarter fleck) and the hard maple are dense, durable, domestic woods that shape beautifully. The maple was textured throughout for visual diversity, an alternative to exotic grain. The oversized leaves recall my experience of once using leaves as umbrellas in a rainforest in which it was actually raining. Those leaf umbrellas were actually quite a bit larger than the ones on this table.

My family recently planted several cherry and maple trees, returning lumber of the same species back to the environment.

Peter Spadone

b. 1955
Kennebunk, Maine

Guardian, 1993
Birch veneer, redwood root burl, pearwood,
basswood, silver leaf, acrylic paint, lacquer
48 x 26 x 13"

As I researched and sought "good wood" for
this project, I was thinking about wildlife as
habitat. The two are inseparable. When timber
is cut, indigenous cultures and traditional forest
uses are affected, and wildlife is forever changed.

The loss of our wild places is the inspiration for
Guardian. The carved snake is as fragile as the
forest she keeps. She is a venomous temple
viper and, to the Hindus who worship her, she
is a deity. Throughout Asia, temple vipers are
kept in a semiwild state. It is common to see
several of them coiled around the head of Shiva
as the worshippers offer rice and sweets, which
attract the mice that sustain the serpents.

All wood use has an impact on wilderness and
diversity, and it is difficult to think of managing
other forests when our own are so poorly
managed, as in the Pacific Northwest. The cliché
"Think globally, act locally" was my guide in
choosing the wood for this piece. I used birch
and birch veneer as the core for the black
lacquer. The redwood root-burl veneer and the
pearwood columns are visual proof of the value
and beauty of temperate wood species and an
affirmation of our need to manage them.

Seth Stem

b. 1947
Providence, Rhode Island

Box With Fifteen Lids, 1993
Maple, bubinga, aniline dye
5 x 22 x 12"
Lent by Elizabeth Isaacson

Wood has tremendous power and influence. More objects, both decorative and utilitarian, are made of wood than any other material. Furthermore, a host of modern materials and applications have evolved that have the appearance of wood, such as the wood-grain plastic laminate that makes a tabletop look like rosewood or the photosynthesized molded plastic that makes the dashboard trim of a car look like walnut.

Perhaps a synthetic material is more valuable if it resembles wood, but I think that the proliferation of fake wood products makes the material seem more common. Much of the wood mimicry is of those species rich in color, texture, and grain, such as rosewood, mahogany, or walnut. This continuous "advertising" further promotes the popularity of a narrow range of well-known and overused species.

In response to this issue, this piece attempts to address perception. Through the use of design elements and factors like color and composition, I have altered the perceived value of two wood species. *Box With Fifteen Lids* has one lid made of maple, bordered by fourteen others made of bubinga. The maple lid is centered in the composition, and, because there is a marked contrast in color between the light maple and the reddish brown bubinga, the eye perceives the maple as the most important element. Through the design, therefore, I have downgraded the importance of a very distinctive, expensive, and endangered species of wood and have given greater importance to an ordinary species of domestic hardwood.

We have the means to manipulate our perception of a material, downplaying or accentuating its value. If more importance is given to common wood species, perhaps there will be some relief for those that are endangered.

Bob Stocksdale

b. 1913
Berkeley, California

Pink Ivory Bowl, 1992
Pink ivory wood, epoxy, lamp black, lacquer
7" h., 10" dia.
Lent by Sylvia and Eric Elsesser

These letters are from Mike Tisdale of
Homestead, Florida. His home and one of his
wood sheds were blown away by Hurricane
Andrew, but his pink ivory logs were still there.

Dear Mr. Stocksdale,
See what you can do with this. It has a
heavy transitional wood between the heart
and sapwood, so you'll have to turn it
pretty good to get to the bright pink.
It may have some nice figure. The dead
branch was most likely killed off in a bush
fire, a drought or by lightning, then the
secondary branch became dormant, which
would cause some pretty compression
lines. It had a hard life—the yellow
discoloration is caused by stress, such as
wind. The deep purple streaks are caused
by fungus and the brown transitional wood
means the tree was dying before the
heartwood could fill the cells with the
extractives that make it pink. Bring it back
to life if you can. —MST

Tisdale sent me a fork from a large tree, from
which I turned three bowls, one inside the
other. I sent him one in thanks for the wood.

Dear Mr. Stocksdale,
When I looked at the slides with the three
pink ivory bowls I wondered who else you
were getting pink ivory from. That's what I
call utilization. I don't think many turners
can keep something like that crotch
together (ingrown bark and all), much less
get three vessels from it.... I enjoyed the
challenge of gathering these old pink ivory
logs as much as you must enjoy revealing
what's inside them. I don't think pink ivory
of this quality will be available for ninety

years or more, not until some of the
young trees get old enough to develop the
pink heart.... While harvesting these old
logs, I thought that they have seen much

over their life. Big pink ivories are
hundreds of years old. If the timber is
worked to its potential and the piece is
made well, it will always be around. —MST

Ross Straker

b. 1953
Hobart, Tasmania, Australia

'Medicine' Drinks Cabinet, 1993
Tasmanian myrtle, myrtle veneer, plywood,
recycled insulin vials, plate glass
19 x 6⁵/₈ x 7"

The forest industry in Tasmania is based on the production of pulpwood for the international market and of saw logs as a byproduct. Large companies are racing to cut as much old-growth forest as they can before plantation-grown eucalyptus becomes available in other countries and the international pulpwood market weakens.

The regeneration of Tasmanian forests is restricted mainly to varieties of eucalyptus and radiata pine, with some small-scale regeneration of blackwood. The current eighty-year, monocultural eucalyptus rotation has a limited future. Minor species cannot become established in these production forests.

A three-hundred-year rotation period is feasible in Tasmania, allowing for complete regeneration of the rainforest and all its diversity. With sensible harvesting and responsible management, the supply of unique local timbers could support a high "value-added" cabinetmaking and craft industry. This added value would far outstrip the fifteen dollars per ton currently received for pulpwood. Such an industry would also create a highly skilled and confident work force.

'Medicine' Drinks Cabinet tackles the issue of rainforest depletion in a number of ways. First, it promotes the value of Tasmanian myrtle and, by extension, other noncommercial species. (Many other species have not yet been assessed for their woodworking qualities.) Second, because the wood is combined with other materials, the cabinet conveys that wood is a precious resource and must be used

sparingly. Third, the technique of using veneers over a plywood substrate is a responsible use of a limited resource and a practical one as well, especially with highly figured or unstable woods.

Finally, this piece refers to the potential benefits of scientific and medical discoveries yet to be made from the largely underresearched temperate rainforests of Tasmania.

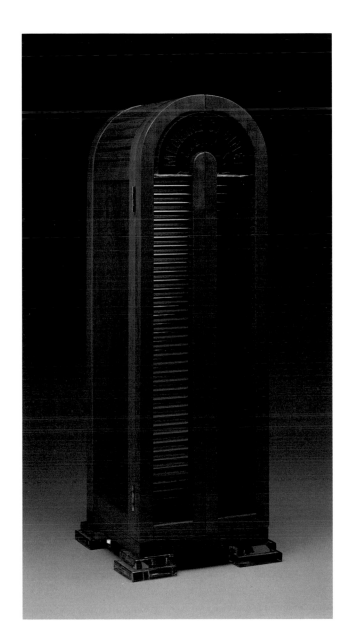

Charles Swanson

b. 1953
New Bedford, Massachusetts

Open-Ended Series #9, 1993
Plaster with acrylic, steel
20 x 84 x 15"

What do we value? Things scarce. Things rare. Things from the past and things that we think will represent a future that may be. We all say that we should stop and smell the roses as we race unseeingly by the wonder of the present, bent on three percent economic growth through a constantly increasing resource consumption.

There is no way to make an object without some environmental impact. My job as a maker is to minimize that impact. I was trained as a woodworker. I laboriously worked small quantities of wood into objects of meticulous craftsmanship. Fifteen years ago, the term "woodworker" was synonymous with "furnituremaker." This is no longer the case. The explosion of materials and techniques has resulted in a variety of work that has surprised even the progenitors of the furniture field.

This piece is the ninth in a series that continues my exploration of a variety of common materials in furniture. It is not environmentally benign. Nothing is. It uses gypsum, which is mined, and steel, which is manufactured. It took electricity to run the welder to connect the metal rods, which most likely burns fossil fuels at its point of generation. Yet it does not directly harm the rainforest. Which is better?

We have to make intelligent choices. Furniture does not have to be made of wood, and mine is certainly not the final exploration of alternative materials. As a society, we have a long history of believing that objects made of common materials are somehow inferior to those made of precious ones. We do not need to continue to believe so. Common materials, manipulated in a thoughtful way, undergo a profound transformation. If we would only look, we would see that their value lies in the preciousness of human creativity.

Michael Swanson

b. 1947
Cobham, Virginia

Chair And Bench, 1993
Ash, cherry, hickory, locust, bark
Chair: 33 x 20 x 14"
Bench: 20 x 20 x 14"

Chairs grow in trees. The fiber and grain of each rung, post, and slat have already reacted to their environment of light and shadow, minerals and rainfall, woodpeckers and borers. Trees branch and curve to the light. A chairmaker molds the naturally curved back posts.

A tree is harvested to allow its neighbors to flourish, and to furnish a house. The wood is selected not only for its quality of sheer strength, shrinkage, beauty, and curve, but also for its relation to the forest. The tree's energy is recycled and unified in a chair.

The chairs I make grow out of the native woods of Albemarle County, Virginia: black ash, pignut, mockerwood hickory, black walnut, black cherry, and locust. The chairmaking process leaves no waste. In the spring, bark is peeled from sap-laden hickory, its sapwood is sectioned out, split, and shaved into rungs. Shavings and heartwood fuel the kiln. Spalting, the edge of decay, represents the continuum of the forest, so it is used as well. It is cyclical work—organic.

The wood is still alive even as the chairs are born, as bent posts shrink over rungs and slats. Shavings burnish the wood, as beeswax from the chairmaker's hives soaks in. Bark is woven and the tension of the forest rhythms fold into the fabric of the chair. Trees grow in chairs.

Roy Tam

b. 1957
Trannon Furniture Ltd.
Pewsey, Wiltshire, England

Hanging Shelf, 1991
Ash thinnings, water-based lacquer
$35^{1}/_{2}$ x $35^{1}/_{2}$ x $5^{1}/_{2}$"

To produce a piece of aluminum requires almost five thousand times the energy required to produce the same volume of timber. Yet wood— the world's only renewable structural material and one of its finest—continues to be ignored by designers in search of high-tech materials.

To grow marketable timber, foresters plant trees close together, discouraging branching. In the competition for light, each tree reaches higher. Before the forest is allowed to mature, four out of five trees are thinned. Forest thinnings are the byproducts of the industry, and an enormous amount of timber is sold for pulp or firewood. The problem for the woodlot owner is that thinning often costs more than the income it generates. For the more marginal thinnings and those felled in difficult terrain, cheaper timber is left to rot.

Hanging Shelf is made from coppiced ash. Coppicing is a method of forestry in which a thicket, or coppice, of small trees is periodically pruned and thinned. The wildlife habitat is undisturbed. The coppice grows vigorously and gives a high yield. But due to the small dimensions of the material, this method has not been popular with industry. This ash was machined in the rough, without splitting and without seasoning the wood. Although 4-in.-diameter ash is too small even for firewood, it makes valuable furniture components.

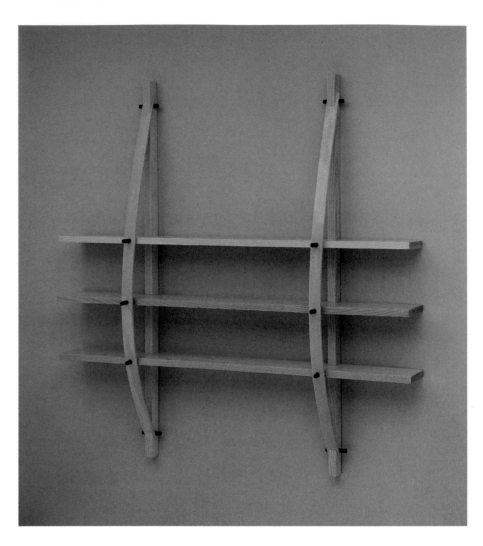

Ninety percent of Britain's timber is imported, yet, every year, almost half of the British timber crop is pulped, burned, or left to rot. The trees sought by industry are tall and branchless, not the gnarled oaks found on the British landscape. If there were a strong demand for coppiced wood, landowners would have to think twice before plowing their woodlands to plant crops.

Richard Tannen
b. 1948
Honeoye Falls, New York

Reliquary 3, 1992
Bleached and dyed ash, lacquer, gold leaf
8¼ x 17 x 4¾"

This box is constructed from ash scraps, left over from other projects. The rough, bandsawn-textured, layering technique allowed the use of material that in both size and quality would not be considered suitable for most fine woodworking. The box is colored with water-based acrylic and finished with water-based lacquer. Further research is needed to determine the environmental impact of gold leaf, but I have applied it as I might an exotic veneer.

This is a secular reliquary. It can hold mementos or souvenirs, but also memories. It offers an opportunity to reflect on a sense of home and family, the precious and the precarious, that which I hold onto and that which I let go. These personal issues parallel environmental issues The earth is our home. All is precious, and most is precarious. What will we hold onto and what will we let go?

Woodworkers are among the most visible ambassadors for the appropriate use of the world's wood products. We give tacit approval to whatever materials and methods we employ. We are all educators and role models in the responsible use of the world's resources.

Peter R. Thibeault
b. 1947
Boston, Massachusetts

Mother's Little Helper, 1993
Medium-density fiberboard, aromatic cedar
flakeboard, oriented-strand board, parallel-
strand lumber, particleboard, Masonite,
water-based adhesives, fillers, finishes
84 x 67 x 18"

This piece is entirely of man-made,
reconstituted wood products, the majority of
which are readily available at any local home
center or lumberyard.

The broom closet and attached ironing-board
table are both supported by turned feet.
The core is medium-density fiberboard and the
interior is aromatic cedar flakeboard, commonly
known as "closet liner." The exterior skin of the
cabinet is made from an engineered structural-
beam material called parallel-strand lumber.
The parquetry is accomplished with book-
matched slices of the end grain, to produce a
textilelike surface. The legs and other turned
parts are made from laminated segments of
oriented-strand board, more commonly known
as "flakeboard." The tabletop and crown are
carved from laminated sheets of particleboard.
The detailing is tempered Masonite. The skin of
the cabinet is sanded and polished to a soft
luster and is left unfinished, as is the interior, to
allow the cedar scent to emerge.

In choosing these materials I am not advocating
their extensive use in the making of fine
furniture. I fully recognize the toxic content of
the glues, binders, and other chemicals used in
their manufacture. Rather, I aim to demonstrate
that there are unique qualities inherent in even
the most common materials and limitless
possibilities for designs that will enhance them.

By illustrating just a few of these design
possibilities, I hope to encourage the "green"
development of those engineered wood
products with specific structural and decorative
applications. Conceivably, all of these products

could be made from sustainable sources, fast-
growing species, recycled materials, and/or
waste and byproducts from other manufacturing
processes. Each new development of technology
adds to our knowledge, knowledge fosters
demand, and greater demand brings lower costs.

The challenge to industry is to develop these
innovative new products in a responsible way.
The artist waits to take the lead in finding
creative ways to use them.

Robert Trotman
b. 1947
Casar, North Carolina

S. Macrophylla, 1987
Mahogany, pigments
15½ x 55 x 26"
Lent by The Society of Arts and Crafts,
Boston, Massachusetts

My piece, *S. Macrophylla,* is certainly politically incorrect. It is made of Honduras mahogany. But it is a piece of mahogany furniture about mahogany furniture, the destruction of the rainforest, and the depletion of this important and beautiful wood.

Much of my work conflates furniture and human forms. Here the two mahogany figures stretch backward in the guise of a bench or low table, as if considering their demise. Their faces are obscured by decorative leaves. The Linnaean designation for mahogany, *Swietenia macrophylla,* is inscribed like an epitaph on their "belly."

Mark Wessinger
b. 1957
New Bedford, Massachusetts

Pedestal Table, 1993
Poplar, glass, acrylic paint
34 x 16 x 16"

This pedestal table is poplar, which I chose for its ability to take paint, its ease in carving, its availability, its low cost, and the fact that its dust does not affect me like that of other woods.

There are approximately thirty-five different species of poplar throughout the Northern Hemisphere. They grow quickly—about 4 to 5 feet a year—and achieve a height of around 60 feet, sometimes as much as 125 feet. Poplars grow straight, with a high crown of branches, and provide plenty of knot-free lumber. Although a poplar's life span is only about seventy-five years, its reproduction is abundant, for the saplings easily sprout from its roots and stumps. Considering the abundance of mature trees and new growth, poplar is a logical choice for sustainable domestic wood.

Instead of using exotic woods, which turn dark in time anyway, I prefer to retain the integrity of my work by using other materials. With paint, I can vary an effect by adding colors or achieve a look not easily attained with natural wood. I painted this piece with water-based acrylics, which are available in a vibrant array of colors, are easy to clean up, and generate no toxic waste.

Ed Zucca
b. 1946
Woodstock, Connecticut

Barkalounger, 1993
Poplar, fir plywood, bark, logs
24 x 84 x 19"

There's nothing nicer than a living tree, except perhaps a lot of trees—big, old trees—and also the sky. You can park your rear end on almost anything if you need to sit down. I admire fine design and craftsmanship, but you can always find better furniture at the Salvation Army than the new stuff. And it's a lot less expensive. Climb down off the juggernaut, save a bag, save a tree, and don't forget to recycle.

*T*he use of lesser-known species from well-managed tropical forests may provide important economic and management tools. Not only can the use of these species help take the pressure off of better-known, overharvested species, but their increased use can enhance the economic value of the whole forest and hence increase the likelihood that it will be maintained as forest.

The long-term success of such a program depends on two factors. Lesser-known species must come from well-managed forests so that they are not simply exploited like their familiar predecessors, and their characteristics and working properties must be fully explored so that they can be connected with the most appropriate end uses. It is to advance this latter goal that the following descriptions have been compiled.

Lesser-Known Species

Key to abbreviations

[M]: Source country and project is Mexico, Plan Piloto Forestal.

[PNG/M]: Source country and project is Papua New Guinea, Masurina.

[PNG/U]: Source country and project is Papua New Guinea, Ulatawa Estates.

Average specific gravity: Density as measured in grams per cubic centimeter

Modulus of rupture (psi): Maximum bending strength

Modulus of elasticity (1000 psi): Degree of stiffness

Maximum crushing strength (psi): Ability to withstand loads parallel to the grain

Volumetric shrinkage: Percentage of shrinkage from green to 12% moisture content

CHAKTÉ, BILLY WEBB *Sweetia panamensis* [M]

Description: Very hard and heavy. Light brown with olive cast, sometimes with darker streaks and golden luster. Fine texture. Roey grain. Sapwood is yellow and clearly distinguishable from the heartwood.

Working properties: Roey grain makes this wood rather difficult to work unless sharp carbide power tools with reduced cutting angles are used. Low silica content. Turns very well, nailing rated poor, screw-holding excellent. Moderately easy to flitch-cut veneer with only slight degrade.

Uses: Heavy construction, handles, flooring, bridge timbers, decorative veneer, turnery, furniture.

Seasoning: Easy to dry with no appreciable degrade. Predrying recommended before kiln-drying. Stable in use.

Average specific gravity: .85
Modulus of rupture (psi): 28,200
Modulus of elasticity (1000 psi): 3,350
Maximum crushing strength (psi): 12,800
Volumetric shrinkage: 12.0%

CHAKTÉ KOK *Sickingia salvadorensis* [M]

Description: Moderately hard and heavy. Heartwood ranges from pale pink orange to bright red and bright reddish orange. Sapwood is clearly distinguishable from the heartwood. Fine texture. Grain is generally straight.

Working properties: Works easily with hand and power tools. Rated excellent in planing, molding, and turning. Rated very poor in nailing and screw-holding.

Uses: Cabinetmaking, inlay, flooring, decorative veneer, fine furniture.

Seasoning: Dries slowly with slight-to-moderate degrade. Controlled predrying before kiln-drying is recommended.

Average specific gravity: .65
Modulus of rupture (psi): 16,200
Modulus of elasticity (1000 psi): 2,420
Maximum crushing strength (psi): 8,600
Volumetric shrinkage: 9.8%

CHECHEM *Metopium brownei* [M]

Description: Hard and heavy. Variegated chocolate brown, reddish brown, with dark streaks and an overall golden luster. Fine texture with long, open, shallow pores. Grain is straight to wavy and roey.

Working properties: Moderately hard to work with hand tools though good results can be achieved using power tools at slow feeds and reduced cutting angles. Finishes smoothly and takes a fine polish.

Uses: Furniture, turnery, inlay, cabinetry, flooring, parquetry, and decorative veneers.

Seasoning: Difficult to dry. Controlled predrying is essential for tolerable level of degrade.

Average specific gravity: .73
Modulus of rupture (psi): 18,400
Modulus of elasticity (1000 psi): 2,400
Maximum crushing strength (psi): 9,350
Volumetric shrinkage: 10.1%

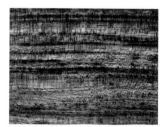

GRANADILLO *Platymiscium af. yucatanum* [M]

Description: Hard and heavy. Dark red to purplish brown, often with purplish streaks and fine parenchyma striping. White sapwood is clearly distinguishable from the heartwood. High luster. Medium texture. Grain is straight to slightly interlocking.

Working properties: Easy to work given the high density of the wood. Very low silica content. Rated excellent in molding and turning. Good in planing. Very poor in nailing and adequate in screw-holding. Takes a high polish.

Uses: Decorative veneers, cabinetry, musical instruments, flooring, turnery, and carvings.

Seasoning: Dries slowly with only slight degrade.

Average specific gravity: .85
Modulus of rupture (psi): 17,200
Modulus of elasticity (1000 psi): 2,200
Maximum crushing strength (psi): 8,700
Volumetric shrinkage: 7.3%

KAMARERE *Eucalyptus deglupta* [PNG/U]

Description: Forest-grown timbers are moderately hard and heavy. Plantation woods are light and soft. Varies from light red to dark reddish brown. Medium texture. Pronounced interlocking grain produces attractive ribbon figure on quarter-sawn surfaces very similar to African mahogany (*Khaya ivorensis*).

Working properties: Easy to work with hand and power tools. Slow planer feed and sharp cutters are needed to avoid pulling grain on quarter-sawn surfaces.

Uses: Flooring, furniture, millwork, and general construction.

Seasoning: Plantation wood is reportedly easy to dry with low degrade. Greater care is needed to dry forest-grown lumber to prevent collapse.

Average specific gravity: .60 (forest grown)/.38 (plantation grown)
Modulus of rupture (psi): 10,550
Modulus of elasticity (1000 psi): 1,530
Maximum crushing strength (psi): 5,650
Volumetric shrinkage: 11.2%

KATALOX *Swartzia cubensis* [M]

Description: One of more than 200 species of *Swartzia*. Very hard and heavy. Dark purplish brown to purplish black. Ivory-colored sapwood is clearly distinguishable from the heartwood. Medium texture. Grain is slightly interlocking.

Working properties: Works easily despite high density. Rated excellent in planing, molding, and turning. Nailing and screw-holding rated poor.

Uses: Cabinetmaking, decorative veneer, interior and exterior construction, high-end furniture, flooring, and parquetry.

Seasoning: Somewhat difficult to dry and with moderate degrade. Slow, controlled predrying recommended before kiln-drying.

Average specific gravity: .85
Modulus of rupture (psi): 21,200
Modulus of elasticity (1000 psi): 2,460
Maximum crushing strength (psi): 11,600
Volumetric shrinkage: 11.8%

KWILA *Intsia bijuga* [PNG/U]

Description: Bright yellow when freshly cut. Turns brown to dark brown. Light yellow sapwood is clearly distinguishable from heartwood. Hard and heavy. Grain is straight to somewhat interlocked. Medium texture. Yellow deposits in the vessels are common.

Working properties: Can be worked with hand and power tools but, because of blunting effect, reduced cutting angles are recommended (20 degrees). Best to treat wood before gluing. Results from staining and finishing are good.

Uses: Boat keels and framing, flooring, furniture, joinery, and decorative veneers.

Seasoning: Seasons well with careful end-sealing. Predrying to 30% moisture content ensures best results.

Average specific gravity: .70 to .85
Modulus of rupture (psi): 20,000
Modulus of elasticity (1000 psi): 2,320
Maximum crushing strength (psi): 9,500
Volumetric shrinkage: 7.8%

MACHICHE, CABBAGE BARK

Lonchocarpus castilloi [M]

Description: Hard and heavy. Yellowish sapwood is clearly distinguishable from the dark chestnut heartwood. Pronounced parenchyma striping. Medium luster. Medium texture. Grain is straight to interlocked.

Working properties: Moderately easy to saw. Planing is difficult with interlocking grain. The high density of the wood makes it hard to work. Tools must be sharp for best results. Very low silica content. Turns very well. Screw-holding is rated excellent.

Uses: Furniture, veneer, turnery, flooring, parquetry, cabinets, paneling.

Seasoning: Drying rate is variable with moderate degrade, which can be minimized if care is taken to slow the drying process.

Average specific gravity: .73
Modulus of rupture (psi): 19,400
Modulus of elasticity (1000 psi): 2,150
Maximum crushing strength (psi): 8,700
Volumetric shrinkage: 12.0%

MERSAWA *Anisoptera costata* [PNG/M]

Description: Moderately hard. Heartwood is a yellowish brown, sometimes with a pinkish cast that fades on drying. Medium texture. Grain is interlocked slightly. Sapwood is not easily distinguished from the heartwood. Rays are prominent on quarter-sawn surfaces, creating a subtle ribbon figure.

Working properties: Silica content is relatively high and will cause blunting of tools (carbide recommended). Finishes smoothly, glues well, stains and finishes well.

Uses: Utility plywood, general construction, furniture, interior joinery, flooring.

Seasoning: Slow drying. Difficult to dry thick stock. Good results can be achieved by careful air-drying before kiln-drying. Only moderate twist encountered when drying.

Average specific gravity: .65
Modulus of rupture (psi): 18,100
Modulus of elasticity (1,000 psi): 1,720
Maximum crushing strength (psi): 8,400
Volumetric shrinkage: 14.6%

NARGUSTA *Terminalia amazonia* [M]

Description: An abundant wood throughout Central and South America. Moderately hard and heavy. Variegated yellow brown to olive brown with prominent reddish stripes. Luster is low on flat-sawn surfaces and medium on quarter-sawn faces. Medium texture.

Working properties: Moderately difficult to work due to grain irregularities. Excellent planing, molding, and turning results when using reduced cutter angles and slow feeds. Nailing is excellent. Screw-holding is fair. Glues and stains well and polishes to a high finish.

Uses: Boatbuilding, plywood, decorative veneer, furniture, turnery, tool handles, truck beds, and flooring.

Seasoning: Somewhat difficult to dry. Moderate degrade even with mild kiln schedules.

Average specific gravity: .76
Modulus of rupture (psi): 26,200
Modulus of elasticity (1000 psi): 2,910
Maximum crushing strength (psi): 11,600
Volumetric shrinkage: 13.3%

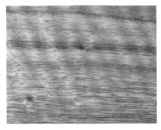

NARRA *Pterocarpus indicus* [PNG/M]

Description: Heartwood is light yellow, yellowish brown to blood red. Whitish sapwood is clearly distinguishable from heartwood. Moderately hard and heavy. Texture ranges from moderately coarse to fine. Grain is often wavy or crossed and gives rise to mottled, fiddleback, ripple, and curly figure. The burl is striking and marketed as Amboyna Burl.

Working properties: Easily worked with hand or power tools. Straight-grained material causes a slight dulling effect on cutters. Treatment of glue joints is recommended.

Uses: Musical instruments, furniture, cabinetry, flooring, turnery, decorative veneers.

Seasoning: Dries slowly but with little degrade. The red woods are more prone to defect and require more care in drying than the yellow varieties.

Average specific gravity: .65
Modulus of rupture (psi): 14,200
Modulus of elasticity (1000 psi): 1,700
Maximum crushing strength (psi): 7,900
Volumetric shrinkage: 7.0%

PNG RED CEDAR *Cedrela toona* [PNG/U]

Description: A mostly light and soft wood. Pale brown to dark reddish brown. Spicy odor. Grain ranges from straight to roey. Quarter-sawn surfaces exhibit attractive rays and high luster. Medium texture is sometimes uneven.

Working properties: Works well with sharp tools. Sometimes difficult to achieve a smooth finish with pronounced roey grain. Glues, stains, and finishes well.

Uses: Boatbuilding and accessories (oars and masts), decorative veneers, doors, musical instruments, cabinetry, and furniture.

Seasoning: Fast drying. Controlled drying minimizes cupping, warping, and surface-checking. Kiln-drying is important to stabilize wood and avoid the exuding of resins in use (except as chest and cabinet linings).

Average specific gravity: .45
Modulus of rupture (psi): 10,600
Modulus of elasticity (1000 psi): 1,300
Maximum crushing strength (psi): 3,480
Volumetric shrinkage: 10.8%

TAUN *Pometia pinnata* [PNG/U]

Description: Moderately hard and heavy. Light to dark reddish brown and often lustrous. Texture ranges from medium to somewhat coarse. Grain is usually straight, sometimes interlocked or wavy.

Working properties: Works easily with hand and power tools. Gluing is reported to be satisfactory. Responds very well to stains and finishes and results in a smooth, fine finish.

Uses: General construction, moldings, paneling, flooring, furniture, interior trim, boatbuilding, decorative veneer, and cabinetry.

Seasoning: Great care is required in drying. Controlled predrying is essential to minimize warping, splitting, and collapse.

Average specific gravity: .70
Modulus of rupture (psi): 15,400
Modulus of elasticity (1000 psi): 2,080
Maximum crushing strength (psi): 8,670
Volumetric shrinkage: 13.2%

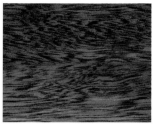

WILD TAMBRAN *Pithecolobium arboreum* [M]

Description: Very hard and heavy. Heartwood is dark golden brown. Sapwood is a light chestnut color, clearly distinguishable from the heartwood. Medium luster. Medium to fine texture. Grain is straight to interlocked with pronounced ribbon figure on quarter-sawn faces.

Working properties: Easy to work with hand and power tools despite high density. Finishes well and takes a high polish.

Uses: Fine furniture, shuttles, cabinetry, tool handles, heavy construction, decorative veneer, flooring, and turnery.

Seasoning: Dries slowly with very little degrade. Dimensionally stable in use.

Average specific gravity: .78
Modulus of rupture (psi): 18,100
Modulus of elasticity (1000 psi): 2,100
Maximum crushing strength (psi): 8,900
Volumetric shrinkage: 7.6%

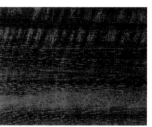

Mechanical Properties of Some U.S. Woods (12% moisture content)

	Specific Gravity	Modulus of Rupture	Modulus of Elasticity	Maximum Crushing Strength	Volumetric Shrinkage
Black walnut	.55	14,600	1,680	7,580	12.8
Butternut	.38	8,100	1,180	5,110	10.6
Cherry	.50	12,300	1,490	7,110	11.5
Sugar maple	.63	15,800	1,830	7,830	14.7
Sugar pine	.36	8,200	1,190	4,460	7.9
White oak	.68	15,200	1,780	7,440	16.3

Mechanical Properties of Some Imported Woods

African ebony	.82	27,400	2,560	13,350	7.0
Balsa	.17	2,800	550	1,700	10.8
Bigleaf mahogany	.50	11,600	1,510	6,630	8.6

References

Benitez Ramos, Rene, and Montesinos Lagos, J.L. 1988. *Catalogo de Cien Especies Forestales de Honduras.* Siguatepeque, Honduras: Escuela Nacional de Ciencias Forestales.

Kribs, David A. 1968. *Commercial Foreign Woods on the American Market.* New York: Dover Publications Inc.

Lincoln, William A. 1991. *World Woods in Color.* Fresno, Calif: Linden Publishing Inc.

Torelli, N. 1983. *Estudio Promocional de 43 Especies Forestales Tropicales Mexicanas.* Mexico City, Mexico: Subsecretaria Forestal, S.A.R.H.

United States Forest Service. 1988. *Dry Kiln Schedules for Commercial Woods / Temperate and Tropical.* U.S. Department of Agriculture Gen. Tech. Report FPL-GTR-57. Washington, D.C.

————. 1974. *Wood Handbook.* Forest Products Laboratory, U.S. Department of Agriculture No. 72. Washington, D.C.

————. 1984. *Tropical Timbers of the World.* U.S. Department of Agriculture Handbook No. 607. Washington, D.C.

Wood samples were supplied by Sea Star Trading of Newport, Oregon, and EcoTimber International of San Francisco, California.

Information was compiled by John Curtis, The Luthier's Mercantile, Healdsburg, California.

Suppliers of Good Wood

This list was compiled by the Woodworkers Alliance for Rainforest Protection (WARP). To the best of its knowledge, all of the following suppliers sell some wood from a well-managed or recycled source, but many of them also carry material from other (unknown) sources. Only those sources that have been designated as "certified" have been evaluated and approved by a certifying agency. New sources and suppliers are occasionally added or deleted. For regular updates, contact WARP.

Try to verify the source of whatever wood you purchase, and remember that local wood is not necessarily "good wood." Temperate-zone wood should be held to the same standards as tropical timber. (WARP and RISD do not guarantee any sources or endorse any specific suppliers.)

Tropical Woods

A & M Wood Specialty *[s/v]*
P.O. Box 32040
Cambridge, Ontario
CANADA N3H SM2
(519-653-9322)
Lesser-known hardwoods from Papua New Guinea (PNG)
and Mexico (PPF)

Almquist Lumber *[s]*
100 Taylor Way
Blue Lake, CA 95521
(707-668-5454)
Lesser-known hardwoods from Mexico (PPF)

Appalachian Interiors *[s]*
201 Amy Drive
Maryville, TN 37801
(615-984-4989)
Lesser-known hardwoods from Peru (Y)

Key to abbreviations

Available products:

[p]: plywood

[s]: sawn wood and/or timbers

[v]: veneer

Sources:

[A]: Amacol Ltda. of Portel, Para, Brazil. A certified Smart Wood source for plywood and veneers.

[EP]: El Pan, a community-based forestry project in Ecuador.

[MOZ]: An integrated resource-management program on the Mocimboa da Praia Biosphere Reserve and a small research program operated by the Mozambique government/Rio Rivuma Low Impact Forest Technology Research Project in Sofala.

[PC]: The Pitsawyers Cooperative in Honduras, a certified Smart Wood source.

[PNG]: Community-based forestry operations in Papua New Guinea, certified by Smart Wood.

[PPF]: Plan Piloto Forestal, a community-based forestry project in Quintana Roo, Mexico. Portions of the PPF have been certified by Scientific Certification Systems (SCS) and Smart Wood.

[Y]: Yanesha Cooperative, a community-based forestry project in the Palcazu Valley of Central Peru.

Berea Hardwoods *[s]*
6367 Eastland Road
Brook Park, OH 44142
(216-234-7949)
Lesser-known hardwoods from Mexico (PPF)

Buchner Design Studios *[s/v]*
1030 Quesada Avenue
San Francisco, CA 94124
(415-822-7300)
Lesser-known tropical hardwoods

Crosscut Hardwoods *[s]*
3065 Front Avenue NW
Portland, OR 97210
(503 224-9663)
Lesser-known hardwoods from Mexico (PPF)

Cut & Dried Hardwoods *[s]*
143 Cedros
Solana Beach, CA 92075
(619-481-0442)
Lesser-known hardwoods from Mexico (PPF)

EcoTimber International *[s]*
P.O. Box 882461
San Francisco, CA 94188
(415-864-4900)
Nonexclusive Smart Wood distributor of lesser-known
hardwoods from Papua New Guinea (PNG) and
Mexico (PPF)

Edensaw Woods *[s]*
211 Seton Road
Port Townsend, WA 98368
(800-950-3336)
Lesser-known hardwoods from Mexico (PPF) and Peru (Y)

EnviResource *[s/v]*
110 Madison Avenue North
Bainbridge Island, WA 98110
(206-842-9785)
Lesser-known tropical hardwoods

Handloggers Hardwood *[s]*
135 East Sir Francis Drake Boulevard
Larkspur, CA 94935
(415 461-1180)
Lesser-known hardwoods from Papua New Guinea (PNG)
and Peru (Y)

I & J Construction *[s/v]*
410 Broadway, Suite B
Santa Monica, CA 90401
(310-395-7533)
Lesser-known tropical hardwoods

Larson Wood Products *[p/v]*
31421 Coburg Bottom Loop
Eugene, OR 97401
(503-343-5229)
Exclusive Smart Wood distributor of Brazilian plywoods and veneers (A) (wholesale only)

Northern Hardwoods *[s]*
520 Matthews Street
Santa Clara, CA 95050
(408-727-2211)
Nonexclusive Smart Wood distributor of lesser-known hardwoods from Papua New Guinea (PNG) and Mexico (PPF)

Pittsford Lumber *[s]*
500 State Street
Pittsford, NY 14534
(716-381-3489)
Lesser-known hardwoods from Mexico (PPF), Peru (Y), and Mozambique (MOZ)

Rio Rivuma *[s/v]*
326 A Street #2C
Boston, MA 02210-1722
(617-451-2549)
Lesser-known and commercial hardwoods from Mozambique (MOZ)

Sea Star Trading *[s/v]*
P.O. Box 513
Newport, OR 97365
(503-265-9616)
Nonexclusive Smart Wood distributor of lesser-known hardwoods from Mexico (PPF)

Tree Products Hardwoods *[s]*
P.O. Box 772
Eugene, OR 97440
(503-689-8515)
Lesser-known hardwoods from Mexico (PPF)

Wildwoods Co. *[s]*
445 I Street
Arcata, CA 95521
(707-822-9541)
Lesser-known hardwoods from Mexico (PPF)

Wilson Woodworks *[s]*
108 Hydeville Road
Stafford, CT 06075
(203-684-9112)
Lesser-known hardwoods from Mexico (PPF)

Wise Wood *[s/v]*
P.O. Box 1271
McHenry, IL 60050
(815-344-4943)
Nonexclusive Smart Wood distributor of lesser-known hardwoods from Papua New Guinea (PNG) and Mexico (PPF)

Woodcastle Forest Products *[s/v]*
34030 Excor Road
Corvallis, OR 97339
(503-926-5488)
Lesser-known tropical hardwoods

Wooden Workbench *[s]*
202-B Airpark Drive
Fort Collins, CO 80524
(303-484-2423)
Lesser-known hardwoods from Mexico (PPF) and Peru (Y)

Woodworkers Source *[s]*
5402 South 40th Street
Phoenix, AZ 85040
(800-423-2450)
Lesser-known hardwoods from Mexico (PPF) and Peru (Y)

Domestic, Recycled and Salvaged Woods

Bronx 2000
1809 Carter Avenue
Bronx, NY 10457
(718-731-3931)
Recycled pallet wood

Byers & Son
P.O. Box 449
Trinidad, CA 95570
(707-822-9007)
Recycled lumber

Caldwell Building Wreckers
195-B Bayshore Boulevard
San Francisco, CA 94124
(415-550-6777)
Recycled lumber

Collins Pine Co. *[s]*
P.O. Box 796
Chester, CA 96020
(916-258-2111)
Certified State-of-the-Art Well-Managed Forest (SCS) (wholesale only)

Duluth Timber Co.
3310 Minnesota Avenue
Duluth, MN 55802
(218-727-2145)
Recycled lumber

Michael Evenson
P.O. Box 191
Redway, CA 95560
(707-923-2979)
Recycled lumber

Florida Ridge
4114 Bridges Road
Groveland, FL 34736-9604
(904-787-4251)
Recycled lumber

Forest Trust Wood Products Brokerage *[s]*
Box 519
Santa Fe, NM 87504
(505-983-8992)
Lumber and Southwest specialty building supplies

Warren Fullmer *[s]*
11750 Hillcrest Road
Medford, OR 97504
(503-772-8577)
Portable, specialty logging and milling. Certified by the Rogue Institute

Goodwin Heart Pine Co. *[s]*
Route 2, Box 119-AA
Micanopy, FL 32667
(800-336-3118)
Newly milled lumber from river-salvaged heart pine

Into the Woods
300 North Water Street
Petaluma, CA 94952
(707-763-0159)
Recycled lumber

The Joinery Company
P.O. Box 518
Tarboro, NC 27886
(919-823-3306)
Recycled lumber

Menominee Tribal Enterprises *[s]*
P.O. Box 10
Neopit, WI 54135
(715-756-2311)
Certified well-managed forest (SCS)

Mountain Lumber
P.O. Box 289
Ruckersville, VA 22968
(804-985-3646)
Recycled lumber

Recycle the Barn People
P.O. Box 294
St. Peter's, PA 19470
(215-286-5600)
Recycled lumber

Sourcebank
1325 Imola Avenue West, #109
Napa, CA 94559
(707-226-9582)
Recycled lumber

SuperTech Woods, Inc. *[v]*
P.O. Box 242
Schoolcraft, MI 49087
(616-323-3570)
Synthesized wood products (EBON-X)

Tosten Brothers *[s]*
P.O. Box 156
Miranda, CA 95553
(707-943-3093)
Hardwood and softwood lumber from private lands

Wild Iris Forestry *[s]*
P.O. Box 1423
Redway, CA 95560
(707-923-2344)
[Sales temporarily suspended during expansion]

British Suppliers

Ecological Trading Company *[s/v]*
659 Newark Road
Lincoln LN6 8SA UK
(011-44-0-522-501-850)
Lesser-known hardwoods from Papua New Guinea (PNG),
Mexico (PPF), Peru (Y), and Honduras (PC)

Milland Fine Timber Ltd. *[s/v]*
The Working Tree
Milland, Nr. Liphook
HANTS GU30 7JS UK
(011-44-0-42-876-505)
Lesser-known hardwoods from Papua New Guinea (PNG),
Mexico (PPF), Peru (Y), Honduras (PC), and Ecuador (EP)

Certifiers of Forest Products

Ecoforestry Institute Society
P.O. Box 5783, Station B
Victoria, British Columbia
Canada V8R 6S8
(604-598-2363)

Forest Trust
P.O. Box 519
Santa Fe, NM 87504

Institute for Sustainable Forestry
P.O. Box 1580
Redway, CA 95560
(707-923-4719)
Pacific Certified Ecological Forest Products

Rainforest Alliance
65 Bleecker Street
New York, NY 10012-2420
(212-677-1900)
Smart Wood

Rogue Institute for Ecology and Economy
P.O. Box 3213
Ashland, OR 97520
(503-482-6031)
Community Forestry

Scientific Certification Systems (SCS)
1611 Telegraph Avenue, Suite 1111
Oakland, CA 94612-2113
(510-832-1415)
Green Cross

Silva Forest Foundation
P.O. Box 9
Slocan Park, British Columbia
Canada V0G 2E0
(604-226-7222)

SGS Silviconsult Ltd.
Magdalen Centre
The Oxford Science Park
Oxford OX4 4GA UK
(011-44-865-784-108)

Soil Association
86 Colston Street
Bristol BS1 5BB UK
(011-44-272-290-661)

Sources of Information

The Forest Partnership
P.O. Box 426
Burlington, VT 05401
(802-863-6789)
Developers of the Forest Resource Information System
(FORIS).

Forest Stewardship Council (FSC)
P.O. Box 849
Richmond, VT 05477
(802-434-3101)
A coalition of representatives from a diverse group of
environmental organizations, human-rights groups,
indigenous peoples' organizations, forest industries,
governments, community forestry projects, and certification
agencies. Sets international standards for forest
management and wood certifiers.

Woodworkers Alliance for Rainforest
Protection(WARP)
One Cottage Street
Easthampton, MA 01027
(413-586-8156)
Reports on certification efforts and updates Good Wood list
in its quarterly journal, Understory.

The Essayists

Edward S. Cooke, Jr., is Charles F. Montgomery Associate Professor of American Decorative Arts at Yale University, New Haven, Connecticut. He was formerly associate curator of American decorative arts and sculpture, the Museum of Fine Arts, Boston, Massachusetts. Cooke has written extensively on both historical and contemporary furniture. He wrote the exhibition catalogues for *New American Furniture: Second Generation Studio Furnituremakers* and *Fiddlebacks and Crooked-backs: Elijah Booth and Other Joiners in Newtown and Woodbury, 1750-1820*. He edited and contributed to *Upholstery in America and Europe from the 17th Century to World War I* and contributed to *Furniture by Wendell Castle* and *"The Art that is Life": The Arts and Crafts Movement in America, 1875-1920*.

Roy Keene is a resource consultant and a former logger and timber broker in Eugene, Oregon. He is founder and executive director of the Public Forestry Foundation (PFF), which promotes prudent public forestry in the Pacific Northwest and specializes in citizen forester education, forestry workshops, analysis, and monitoring. Keene has written widely about Northwest forestry issues and he edits the quarterly PFF journal, *The Public Forester*.

Silas Kopf has an undergraduate degree in architecture from Princeton University, Princeton, New Jersey. He spent a two-year apprenticeship with Wendell Castle in Rochester, New York. In 1988 he received a fellowship from the National Endowment for the Arts to study traditional marquetry techniques at l'Ecole Boulle in Paris. He has had three one-man exhibitions in New York City and has had numerous pieces in national shows, including the touring exhibition *Art That Works*. Since 1978, Kopf has operated his own furnituremaking and marquetry studio in Northampton, Massachusetts, and he is a founding director of the Woodworkers Alliance for Rainforest Protection.

Scott Landis is a writer, editor, and photographer specializing in woodworking-craft traditions, forest management, and wood-use issues. The author of *The Workbench Book, The Workshop Book*, and numerous essays and articles, Landis is a founding director and president of the Woodworkers Alliance for Rainforest Protection and editor of the quarterly WARP journal, *Understory.* He is working on a book about the "industrial ecology" of American mahogany and its historic role in trade, design, and modern forest management.

John Makepeace is a British furniture designer and educator whose work has been extensively reviewed in books and magazine articles and on television in England and around the world. Trained as a cabinetmaker in the 1950s, his work has appeared in dozens of exhibitions in England, Canada, Japan, Germany, Belgium, Spain, and the United States. Makepeace is a fellow of the Royal Society of Arts, director of the Parnham Trust, and a former trustee of the Victoria and Albert Museum (1988-1991). In 1988, he was awarded Order of the British Empire (OBE) in recognition of his services to furniture design.

Robert O'Neal received his bachelor of science degree from Philadelphia College of Art (1962) in Pennsylvania, and his master's degree from Cornell University (1973), Ithaca, New York. He also studied at the Academy André l'Hote and l'Ecole des Beaux Arts in Paris, France. O'Neal has shown work at Gallery 91 in New York City, the Gallery of Architecture in Baltimore, Maryland, the Gallery NAGA in Boston, Massachusetts, and has exhibited drawings in the Decorative Art Wing of the Louvre in Paris. He has published articles in *ID* magazine, *Axis,* the Japanese design magazine, and *The Design Educator's Prospectus.* O'Neal is a practicing designer and professor in the Department of Industrial Design at Rhode Island School of Design.

Laura K. Snook specialized in tropical forestry at the Yale School of Forestry and Environmental Studies, Yale University, New Haven, Connecticut, where she earned her master's degree (1980) and doctorate (1993) in forest science. Between 1980 and 1986 she worked on rural-development forestry, natural forest management, forest-habitat conservation, and deforestation dynamics in Mexico as a professor and researcher at the National Institute for Research on Biotic Resources. She carried out her doctoral research on the ecology and management of the mahogany forests of the Yucatan peninsula and has also worked on extractive reserves and other aspects of forestry in the Brazilian Amazon.

Seth Stem received his bachelor of fine arts degree in landscape architecture from Pennsylvania State University (1970), State College, Pennsylvania, and his master of fine arts degree in furniture design from Virginia Commonwealth University (1980) in Richmond, Virginia. An associate professor in the Industrial Design Department of Rhode Island School of Design since 1980, Stem is the author of *Designing Furniture.* His work has been shown extensively in galleries and museums across the United States and he is presently designing production furniture for American furniture companies and Southeast Asian manufacturers.

Timothy J. Synnott lives in Saltillo, Mexico, and specializes in the management, silviculture, and ecology of natural tropical forests. A forestry graduate from Oxford University (1965), Oxford, England, Synnott worked for eight years in Uganda, first as a forest manager and then as a student of the natural regeneration of African mahoganies. He obtained his doctorate in 1976 from Makerere University, Uganda, and has taught and conducted research in tropical and subtropical forestry and in plantations in forty countries. He has consulted a wide variety of forestry and rural-development projects in Africa, South America, and Asia and he recently launched a new environmental program in Latin America for the Overseas Development Agency.

Edward O. Wilson is a professor at the Museum of Comparative Zoology, Harvard University, Cambridge, Massachusetts. An authority on social insects, Wilson was one of the creators of the theory of island biogeography, which examined the relationship of size to biological diversity in the world's threatened rainforests. He is the author of numerous books, essays, and articles, including *On Human Nature,* which won the Pulitzer Prize in 1979, *Sociobiology: The New Synthesis,* and *The Diversity of Life.*

The Makers

Mitchell Ackerman, *Providence, Rhode Island*

Peter Adams, *Hobart, Tasmania, Australia*

Fred Baier, *Pewsey, Wiltshire, England* ✉

Bruce Beeken, *Shelburne, Vermont*

Garry Knox Bennett, *Oakland, California* ✉

Henry Black, *Concord, New South Wales, Australia*

Michael Brolly, *Hamburg, Pennsylvania*

Jon Brooks, *New Boston, New Hampshire* ✉

Arthur Espenet Carpenter, *Bolinas, California* ✉

Polly Cassel, *Northampton, Massachusetts*

Martha Chatelain, *Rancho Santa Fe, California*

Il Sang Cho, *Pusan, Korea* ✉

Stephen Daniell, *Easthampton, Massachusetts*

John Dunnigan, *West Kingston, Rhode Island* ✉

David Ebner, *Bellport, New York*

David Ellsworth, *Quakertown, Pennsylvania* ✉

Glenn Elvig, *Minneapolis, Minnesota*

J. Paul Fennell, *Topsfield, Massachusetts*

David Fobes, *San Diego, California*

Eck Follen, *New Bedford, Massachusetts* ✉

W. Logan Fry, *Richfield, Ohio*

Dewey Garrett, *Livermore, California*

Eric Gesler, *Enfield, New Hampshire*

Hank Gilpin, *Lincoln, Rhode Island* ✉

Carolyn Grew-Sheridan, *San Francisco, California*

John Grew-Sheridan, *San Francisco, California*

Kenton D. Hall, *Muncie, Indiana*

Stephen Hogbin, *Owen Sound, Ontario, Canada* ✉

Richard Hooper, *Liverpool, Merseyside, England*

Michael Hosaluk, *Saskatoon, Saskatchewan, Canada* ✉

Dwight N. Huffman, *Ithaca, New York*

Dean Johnston, *Kahului, Hawaii*

Thomas Kamila, *Ashburnham, Massachusetts*

Silas Kopf, *Northampton, Massachusetts* ✉

Peter Kovacsy, *Pemberton Western Australia, Australia*

Keith Kutch, *Savannah, Georgia* ✉

William Laskin, *Toronto, Ontario, Canada* ✉

Lucinda Leech, *Oxford, Oxfordshire, England* ✉

Tom Loeser, *Madison, Wisconsin* ✉

Kristina Madsen, *Easthampton, Massachusetts* ✉

John Makepeace, *Beaminster, Dorset, England* ✉

John Marcoux, *Providence, Rhode Island* ✉

Wendy Maruyama, *San Diego, California* ✉

Alphonse Mattia, *Westport, Massachusetts* ✉

Peter Murkett, *Monterey, Massachusetts*

Christoph Neander, *Providence, Rhode Island*

Robert O'Neal, *Rehoboth, Massachusetts*

Jeff Parsons, *Shelburne, Vermont*

Tim Philbrick, *Narragansett, Rhode Island* ✉

John Rantanen, *Ithaca, New York*

Tom Rauschke, *Palmyra, Wisconsin*

Christopher Rose, *Brighton, East Sussex, England*

Mitch Ryerson, *Cambridge, Massachusetts*

Paul Sasso, *Almo, Kentucky* ✉

Kenneth Scherdell, *Worcester, Massachusetts*

Lee Schuette, *Kittery Point, Maine*

Mark Sfirri, *New Hope, Pennsylvania*

John Shipstad, *Coos Bay, Oregon* ✉

Randy Shull, *Asheville, North Carolina*

Naomi Siegmann, *Mexico City, Mexico*

Ron Smith, *Falmouth, Massachusetts*

Rosanne Somerson, *Westport, Massachusetts* ✉

Peter Spadone, *Kennebunk, Maine*

Seth Stem, *Providence, Rhode Island* ✉

Bob Stocksdale, *Berkeley, California*

Ross Straker, *Hobart, Tasmania, Australia*

Charles Swanson, *New Bedford, Massachusetts* ✉

Michael Swanson, *Cobham, Virginia*

Roy Tam, *Pewsey, Wiltshire, England*

Richard Tannen, *Honeoye Falls, New York*

Peter R. Thibeault, *Boston, Massachusetts*

Robert Trotman, *Casar, North Carolina*

Mark Wessinger, *New Bedford, Massachusetts*

Kaaren Wiken, *Palmyra, Wisconsin*

Gary A. Zeff, *Rancho Santa Fe, California*

Ed Zucca, *Woodstock, Connecticut* ✉

✉ Invited Artist

Editorial Director: Scott Landis

Editor: Deborah Cannarella

Designer: Jeanne Criscola

Production: Debra Della Camera and Suzan Shutan

Typefaces: Galliard and Gill Sans

Printer: W.E. Andrews

Paper: 100 lb., Consort Royal Osprey Silk Text and Brilliance Cover. These premium papers are acid free and contain a minimum of fifty percent of recycled fiber, including at least ten percent of de-inked, postconsumer waste. No fluorescent dyes or chlorine bleach have been used in manufacturing process.

Consort Royal Osprey is manufactured at the Donside Paper Mill in Aberdeen, Scotland, which generates all of its heat and power by hydroelectricity and North Sea natural gas. All water used in the paper's production is processed through Aberdeen's municipal sewage-treatment system before disposal. Donside's operations and environmental controls have been certified for total quality management by the International Standards Organization (ISO).

(Consumer demand for chlorine-free paper will encourage the pulp-and-paper industry to choose more environmentally sound processes. For information regarding Consort Royal Osprey, call UK Paper North America, Inc., 1-800-220-8577.)